CAN YOU SCORE
IN FOOTBALL KNOWLEDGE?

Name the All-AFL halfback who admits, "I like to humiliate my man by faking him. . . ."

Which NFL quarterback set an all-time single-season completion record in 1967?

Leroy Kelly took "the biggest gamble a halfback can take last season." What was it?

As soon as the NFL championship game ended, which Cowboy superstar was preparing to start practicing for the '68 season?

"I learned what it's like to be a marked man . . . ," an All-AFL runner said at the end of last season. Name him.

Name the NFL receiver who, after catching only 35 passes in four years, caught 63 in '67?

IF YOU ANSWERED THESE QUESTIONS CORRECTLY, you've scored the tying touchdown. Add the winning point by identifying the halfback who in only his third season led one top scout to say about him: "He's in the Hall of Fame already."

IF YOU HAVEN'T ANSWERED ALL THESE QUESTIONS, you'll find the answers in FOOTBALL STARS OF 1968, in exciting stories and up-to-date facts that are presented to make this the most thrilling season you've ever followed.

BERRY STAINBACK, Managing Editor of *Sport Magazine*, is the author of BASKETBALL STARS OF 1968, also published by Pyramid, and five other books. He lives with his wife, Rita, and children, Dawn, age 10, and Deron, age 8, in North Tarrytown, New York.

FOOTBALL
STARS
of 1968

BERRY STAINBACK

PYRAMID BOOKS NEW YORK

To my nephews,
Jack Hourigan and Mike Hourigan,
who dig the game.

FOOTBALL STARS OF 1968

A PYRAMID BOOK
First printing August, 1968

Copyright © 1968 by Pyramid Publications, Inc.

PYRAMID BOOKS are published by Pyramid Publications, Inc.,
444 Madison Avenue, New York, New York 10022, U.S.A.

TABLE OF CONTENTS

THE SUPER BOWL

Willie Davis, Green Bay's great veteran defensive end said what the Super Bowl was all about in the locker room afterward: "I'll tell you about a game like this—there are three things. First, it's the pride and reputation of the NFL against the AFL. Second, it's the challenge of winning the game twice. And third, it's the money."

The money, as it had been the previous year, was good: $15,000 to every member of the winning team, $7500 to every member of the losing team. But like the previous year, it was strictly a one-half football game. In the second half of the '66 game against Kansas City, the Packers simply swallowed the Chiefs whole. The Packers did the same thing to the Oakland Raiders in '67.

After Green Bay had gone ahead 13-0, Oakland came back with a Daryle Lamonica-to-Bill Miller touchdown pass. Then the Packers kicked a field goal with only seconds left in the half. But in the second half Green Bay scored 17 points and held the Raiders to another 23-yard touchdown reception by Miller.

The outstanding player of the game for the second successive year was Green Bay quarterback Bart Starr, who completed 13 of 24 passes for 202 yards and a touchdown. He also directed the drives that set up four field goals by Don Chandler. Starr received a Corvette from *Sport Magazine* for his MVP performance, but donated the car to a children's home.

NATIONAL FOOTBALL LEAGUE

Fittingly, the most exciting game of the 1967 NFL season was the one between the Dallas Cowboys and the Green Bay Packers for the championship. Playing at Lambeau Field in Green Bay in 13-below-zero temperatures, the Packers were trying to become the first team in league history to win three successive world titles. They started off as they had the previous year, scoring 14 points before the Cowboys could get started. Quarterback Bart Starr threw an eight-yard touchdown pass to his flanker, Boyd Dowler, in the first quarter, then hit him with a 46-yard bomb in the second quarter.

Suddenly, though, the tide turned. The Cowboy rush line began blasting in on Starr and Willie Townes dropped him for a 17-yard loss, causing Bart to fumble. George Andrie of the Cowboys scooped up the ball and carried it seven yards into the end zone. The Packer lead was cut to 14-7.

Meanwhile the Green Bay defense was completely throttling the Dallas offense, putting pressure on Cowboy quarterback Don Meredith and stopping his ground game. Even when Meredith found time to throw he passed badly in the extremely cold weather, completing only four of 13 passes in the first half. However, the Cowboys managed to score again after they forced Packer safetyman Willie Wood to fumble a punt, which they recovered. Danny Villanueva kicked a 21-yard field goal.

The third quarter was scoreless as the defenses of each team took turns dominating the action. Starr in particular was harassed by a Cowboy front four that beat the cold by beating him down. All told, Starr was dropped eight times for losses totaling 76 yards.

Early in the fourth quarter Meredith finally got a drive going. It carried to mid-field and Meredith called on halfback Dan Reeves for an option pass. He swept right, the Packers moved up to stop him, and Cowboy flanker Lance Rentzel was left all alone. He caught the pass and scored. For the first time in the game, the Cowboys had the lead.

Starr had plenty of time to overcome the 17-14 deficit, but he couldn't sustain anything until the Packers took over the ball for the last time with five minutes left to play. Relying mostly on passes to his running backs, Bart moved the team to the Cowboy one. There were only 13 seconds on the clock and no time-outs left when Starr snuck into the end zone for the winning touchdown.

"It would have been close," Vince Lombardi said afterward when asked if he thought the Packers could have tried a field goal had the sneak failed. "We didn't want a tie. We had compassion for those spectators sitting out in that cold all that time. We wanted to send them home right then."

The Packer road to the NFL championship was relatively easy. Despite injuries to Bart Starr that hampered him much of the season and despite injuries to regular running backs Elijah Pitts and Jim Grabowski, Green Bay easily won the Central Division. The Packers had already clinched the title with a 9-3-1 record when they lost the season's final game to Pittsburgh. (Many of the Packer players felt Vince Lombardi wanted to make a point to them before the Western Conference title game; if so, it was a point well-taken.) Second to Green Bay in the Central Division were the Chicago Bears, who introduced a new concept to defensive play that proved highly effective. They used a lot of blitzes, led by middle linebacker Dick Butkus, and a five-man "prevent" secondary on every passing situation. They still had Gale Sayers, the one-man ground game, but an inept passing attack held the Bears to a 7-6-1 record. Right behind them for similar reasons were the Detroit Lions. They had a good, if somewhat inconsistent, defense (rookie cornerback Lem Barney led the league in interceptions with ten, three of which he returned for touchdowns to tie the league record) and a running attack built around Rookie-of-the-Year Mel Farr. But Detroit must build a passing game around ex-Ram Bill Munson. The same can be said of the Minnesota Vikings, 3-8-3 a year ago, with Gary Cuozzo obtained from New Orleans.

The Coastal Division produced the great race of the season (see the Johnny Unitas profile) with the rejuvenated Los Angeles Rams beating the Baltimore Colts in the final game of the season to take the title. They both finished with 11-1-2 records, but the Rams earned the right to lose 28-7 to Green Bay the following week by virtue of the fact that they'd scored more points against Baltimore in their head-to-head meetings. San Francisco started well in the Coastal Division, winning five of six games, including one over the Rams. Then two top 49er ends, Dave Parks and Monty Stickles, were lost for the season, quarterback John Brodie started completing too many passes to the opposition—and San Francisco lost six successive games. Young quarterback George Mira rallied the team to wins in the final two games, but it didn't save coach Jack Christiansen's job. The Atlanta Falcons did worse in their second year than they did in their first, winning one and tying one of 14 games, but coach Norb Hecker did keep his job.

The Eastern Conference races were not races at all. The Cowboys had no competition in the Capitol Division, and neither did the Cleveland Browns in the Century Division. Each had a 9-5 record, and the nearest competitor in the Century was the New York Giants with a 7-7 record. The second-place team in the Capitol Division was the Philadelphia Eagles with an ever worse record, 6-7-1. A quarterback was responsible, for the most part, for the surprising rise of the Giants. He was former Viking Fran Tarkenton, who found the best set of receivers he'd ever worked with and took advantage of them. The Cardinals had surprising early success with young quarterback Jim Hart after regular Charley Johnson was drafted, but Hart wasn't consistent enough to sustain his initial heroics. The Cards finished with a 6-7-1 record, just ahead of the 4-9-1 Steelers, who may have found a good young quarterback in Kent Nix, but who lacked a solid running game.

The most exciting team in football last season, and also the most perplexing, was the Washington Redskins. Ten of their games were decided in the closing moments. They finished 5-6-3, just ahead of the expansion New Orleans Saints, who somehow managed to win three of their 14 games.

In the Eastern Conference championship game, the

Cowboys had an even easier time with the Browns than the Packers did with the Rams for the Western title. Meredith completed ten of 12 passes for 212 yards before retiring, flanker Bob Hayes covered 86 yards with one reception and 64 and 68 with two punt returns—and the Cowboys won 52-14.

AMERICAN FOOTBALL LEAGUE Most so-called pro football experts (including this one) picked the AFL champion Kansas City Chiefs to easily win the Western Division title in '67, and figured the Buffalo Bills would be the best team in the East. So the Bills were never really a factor once the season started and the Chiefs also stumbled badly. However, there were interesting races in both divisions.

The Raiders started right off showing everyone they weren't fooling around, beating Denver 51-0, beating Boston 35-7, and then upsetting Kansas City 23-21. They stumbled the next week in New York, playing a poor game and losing 27-14. But that was the only game they were to lose until the Super Bowl.

Nevertheless, the San Diego Chargers were undefeated in their first five games, including a 45-21 win over Kansas City in which Charger defensive back Speedy Duncan showed his speed on a 100-yard interception return and a 35-yard touchdown run with a fumble. Two weeks later the Chargers, who had been tied by Boston, met the Raiders for first place in the West. In this game Oakland quarterback Daryle Lamonica passed for 316 yards and San Diego quarterback John Hadl passed three times to Raider defensive back Dave Grayson. The final score was 51-10 Raiders ... and the closest game they had through the rest of the season was a 21-17 decision over Denver.

In the meantime the Chiefs, after splitting their first six ball games, won six of their last eight. What was the difference between the Kansas City team of '66 and that of '67? The defensive holes which showed themselves so garishly in the Super Bowl proved just as much a problem last season. Coach Hank Stram tried to shore up his weak corners with two rookies, but inexperience and injuries proved costly. Even the acquisition of giant tackle Ernie Ladd from Houston early in the season did little to improve the Kansas City pass rush until late in the schedule. The Chiefs' strong finish and the fact that San Diego lost its last four games moved Kansas City (9-5) a half-game ahead of the Chargers (8-5-1). The Denver Broncos, in the process of a complete rebuilding by new coach Lou Saban, finished last with a 3-11 record.

In the Eastern Division race, Buffalo opened with a 20-17 win over the New York Jets, but then were shut out by Oakland, 51-0, and lost to the second-year Miami Dolphins, 35-21. Obviously the great Bill defense of other years had slipped considerably, and so had quarterback Jack Kemp. Lamonica was no longer around to bail him out, and the wide end expected to help him so much, Art Powell was sidelined for the season in the early going. So, too, was halfback Bobby Burnett, the '66 Rookie-of-the-Year. Buffalo lost its third game in a row, to San Diego, 37-17, then beat Denver by a point before losing to Oakland and virtually falling out of contention.

Meanwhile, the Jets, following their opening loss to Buffalo, swung into full gear under the leadership of Joe Namath's passing and the running of halfback Emerson Boozer. New York won five and tied one of its next six games to pile up an impressive lead in the East.

Then the Oilers, who were scuffling along with a 4-2-1 record as first Jackie Lee, then Don Trull and Bobby Davis got a shot at quarterback, traded Ernie Ladd to Kansas City for veteran reserve quarterback Pete Beathard. He didn't show the kind of passing coach Wally Lemm expected him to, but Beathard did provide the direction the Oilers needed and the team began to move under the legs of second-year fullback Hoyle Granger (who rushed for over 1000 yards) and rookie halfback Woody Campbell. The Jets lost their legs when speedy Em Boozer was operated on following the November 5 loss to Kansas City. Joe Namath's arm alone was not enough to carry the team. In the next-to-last game of the season the

Oilers beat the Chargers and took the Division lead as the Jets lost the rematch to the Raiders on the Coast.

Houston finished with a 9-4-1 record, the Jets at 8-5-1, the Bills at 4-10. The latter mark tied them with the Miami Dolphins, who avoided last place thanks to the 3-10-1 Boston Patriots. Boston coach Mike Holovak tried to solve his quarterback problems by using both veteran Babe Parilli and young Don Trull (acquired in trade from the Oilers), but it didn't help. Miami coach George Wilson, on the other hand, found himself an excellent-looking quarterback in rookie Bob Griese, who led the Dolphins to three victories in their last five games.

PREVIEW OF THE 1968 SEASON

NATIONAL FOOTBALL LEAGUE

We are pleased to report that our prediction scorecard last season turned out very well in the NFL. (You may have noticed that in other years we neglected to mention our record in such matters; there was ample reason.) The Los Angeles Rams won the Coastal Division, the Green Bay Packers won the Central Division, and the Packers beat the Rams for the Western Conference title, as predicted. In the East we were half-right, picking the Dallas Cowboys to win the Capitol Division, which they did, and the St. Louis Cardinals to win the Century Division, which they didn't, but probably would have if quarterback Charley Johnson hadn't been drafted. Accurate predictions this season will be even tougher because draft boards will be tougher. This is why as we went to press in April there still had been very little trading in either professional league. Teams were simply afraid to make any deals because of the uncertain availability of some of their youngsters.

However, we still plunge ahead with our predictions anyway:

WESTERN CONFERENCE

Central Division	Coastal Division
Green Bay	Baltimore
Chicago	Los Angeles
Detroit	San Francisco
Minnesota	Atlanta

EASTERN CONFERENCE

Capitol Division	Century Division
Dallas	Cleveland
Washington	St. Louis
New York	Pittsburgh
Philadelphia	New Orleans

CENTRAL DIVISION

The GREEN BAY PACKERS—the first team to win three successive world championships—should win their fourth straight NFL title in 1968, and go on to take their third Super Bowl in a row. They are far and away the best team in professional football, despite the fact that the Cowboys have pressed them dearly in the last two National League championship games.

The only thing that seems capable of halting the inexorable Packers is a serious injury to quarterback Bart Starr. Zeke Bratkowski did yeoman service filling in for Starr from 1964 through 1966, but last season the aging Zeke slipped a bit and he's not getting any younger. Vince Lombardi feels he has Starr's eventual replacement in second-year man Don Horn, but he won't blow Starr's sweet tunes on a football field for a few years.

However, barring injury to Starr, the Packers could have their best backfield since the heyday of Paul Hornung and Jim Taylor. Travis Williams, the man the Packer players dubbed "Instant Hero" as a rookie after he'd run back an all-time NFL record four touchdowns in one season, should take over the regular halfback spot. Donny Anderson may be switched to the flank—where he could become another Charley Taylor. And veteran Elijah Pitts, fully recovered from his '67 injury, will take the pressure off Williams. Fullback Jim Grabowski, just coming into his own when he was sidelined last season, will be back and ready to become a top performer in his first full season on the job.

Tight end, a Packer soft spot ever since Ron Kramer went to the Lions in '65, is expected to be filled by number one draft choice Fred Carr. Veterans Carroll Dale, Boyd Dowler and Bob Long are all fine wide receivers. And the Packers have been rebuilding their offensive line as they go along with little loss in efficiency. Gale Gillingham at guard and Bob Hyland at center became regulars last season. Veterans Jerry Kramer, Forrest Gregg and Bob Skoronski remain first-rate.

There isn't much you can say about the magnificent Packer defense except that, if anything, it gets more magnificent yearly. As the great veteran line gets some age on it, two youngsters with tremendous potential, Bob Brown and Jim Weatherwax, paw the dirt on the sideline waiting to get in. There is similarly impressive depth at linebacker (where Jim Flanigan backs up the super trio of Ray Nitschke, Dave Robinson and Lee Roy Caffey) and in the secondary (where John Rowser could push either Tom Brown or, surprise, Herb Adderley for work alongside Bob Jeter and Willie Wood).

Vince Lombardi, you left some *stuff* for Phil Bengtson.

The talent falls off considerably below the Packers in the Central Division. It remains to be seen whether the CHICAGO BEARS' wild new defense that featured five men in the secondary in almost every passing situation last season can be as successful a second time around. We well remember the early success of the 49ers' Shotgun offense—that was quickly caught up to and shot down in 1961. That could be the fate of the Bear defense in '68. But there does seem to be adequate personnel on the unit, led by fine young middle linebacker Dick Butkus.

On offense, though, there remain several problems— primarily the terrifying hole at quarterback. Jack Concannon is a good running quarterback, but he doesn't pass like a professional. Neither did Larry Rakestraw or Rudy Bukich last season. The offensive line is being rebuilt and should do better by Gale Sayers this year, which will help. He may have to be a one-man offense again.

The DETROIT LIONS may have found in Bill Munson, acquired from the Rams, their first consistent quarterback, a task they have been at ever since Bobby Layne left town. Coach Joe Schmidt may also give playing time to number one draft choice Greg Landry over Karl Sweetan. The team is loaded with fine receivers and an outstanding young runner in Mel Farr, plus a capable offensive line. The defense is led by one of the finest secondaries in the league, featuring Dick LeBeau and Lem Barney at the corners. The line, led by Alex Karras, and the linebacking, led by Wayne Walker, is capable—and would doubtless be more consistent if the offense gave them any hope.

The MINNESOTA VIKINGS were disappointed by their potentially fine rookie crop last season, but the key to the team's problems was at quarterback. There was simply no one who could replace the traded-at-his-own-request Fran Tarkenton. Canadian veteran Joe Kapp may do better in his second year in the NFL; Gary Cuozzo, one-time back up to Johnny Unitas could get the regular job. The receivers are there, led by Paul Flately and young Bob Grim, as is the offensive line. The defensive problems which plagued the team during Norm Van Brocklin's time continue to show. But the defensive personnel is better than it has ever been if coach Bud Grant can put it all together.

COASTAL DIVISION

The BALTIMORE COLTS came close to the title last season while they were rebuilding their offensive line. That line was solid most of the year, and should be even better this season. In addition, quarterback John Unitas has a great new weapon in his arsenal—halfback Timmy Brown, acquired from the Eagles for Al Haymond, who lost his job in the secondary after he was injured in '67. Brown is probably the outstanding receiver among running backs in the league—and if he stays healthy there's no reason why he shouldn't have his finest season on the other end of Unitas' passes. What's more, Timmy also provides the outside running speed Baltimore needs to combine with the inside rushing of fullbacks Jerry Hill and Tony Lorick. The Colt defense features no super individuals, but it is an outstanding "team" unit—and Timmy Brown will help take some pressure off it by allowing Unitas to use more of a ball-control offense in '68.

The LOS ANGELES RAMS will again be tough, because coach George Allen has developed a solid all-around ball club. But the difference between the Rams and the Colts, we feel, will lie in the quarterbacking. Certainly no quarterback ever improved more from one season to the next than Roman Gabriel did last year. But we're not firmly convinced he can be as consistently sharp as he was last season. Also, Bernie Casey is his lone outstanding receiver. The defense is mammoth in size and ability up front, but when that front four is checked a bit, the secondary can be passed against.

The SAN FRANCISCO 49ers have a new coach in former Cowboy assistant Dick Nolan, a highly respected football man. Last year the team's main problems were injuries and poor quarterbacking by veteran John Brodie. George Mira seemingly won the job late in the season, and he does appear to have a great facility for moving a ball club. His top receivers, Dave Parks and Sonny Randle, along with tight end Monty Stickles, will be back. The offensive line and running attack are good. So, too, is the defense when the offense gives it time to breathe. If it does, the 49ers could also be in contention.

The ATLANTA FALCONS are a long way from home and in the roughest division in pro football. Which is no help at all to a young team. But coach Norb Hecker is building, and you can be sure the Falcons will win more than one game this season.

CAPITOL DIVISION

Even with quarterback Don Meredith in and out of ball games with injuries last season, the DALLAS COWBOYS were clearly the class in the East. In fact, young Craig Morton was forced to fill in for Meredith, picked up a lot of experience and came on very well. This team now appears to have fine depth at this key position. The team's wide receivers—Bob Hayes, Lance Rentzel and rookie Dennis Homan—and running backs—Danny Reeves and Don Perkins—are excellent. The offensive line has also developed into a first-rate unit. And the defense, though still not as consistent as coach Tom Landry would like, can be as good as any in football. Willie Townes and Jethro Pugh are two fast-improving youngsters who will take some pressure off veterans Bob Lilly and George Andrie in the rush line. All in all, the Cowboys are again the team to beat in the Eastern Conference.

The WASHINGTON REDSKINS have the best quarterback in the East in Sonny Jurgensen, plus the best set of receivers in football—Charley Taylor, Bobby Mitchell and Jerry Smith. Which is why we're picking them as high as second in the Capitol Division. However, for the Redskins to contend, Otto Graham must strengthen his defense and establish an adequate running attack. Apparently Graham feels his number one draft choice of '67, fullback Ray McDonald, will come on. Graham's first two '68 draft picks were a defensive back, Jim Smith of Oregon, and a linebacker, Tom Roussel of Mississippi Southern. They should help.

The NEW YORK GIANTS, like the Redskins, have a quarterback, Fran Tarkenton, and the receivers—Homer Jones, Aaron Thomas and Joe Morrison—they can win with. They also have a fine running back in Ernie Koy, who despite injuries rushed for 704 yards in '67. But with Tucker Frederickson's future as a runner questionable after his second knee operation, the Giants need another solid running back, a more consistent offensive line, and a much improved defense to get into contention. The '67 defense was 100 percent improved over '66, but it still has quite a way to go—particularly in mounting a pass rush.

The PHILADELPHIA EAGLES finally saw quarterback Norm Snead develop into the kind of passer they thought he would be when they traded Sonny Jurgensen for him in '63. Tom Woodeshick developed into a solid runner and Ben Hawkins into a first-rate flanker, but another running back and a top tight end are needed (Mike Ditka will be the man if he's healthy again) for the offense. And the defense needs all kinds of help to improve its pass rush and its coverage in the secondary. Coach Joe Kuharich, assuming he's still there, figures Al Haymond from the Colts will solidify the secondary.

CENTURY DIVISION

The CLEVELAND BROWNS were an amazing team in '67. Despite dissatisfaction by Negro players that saw a mass holdout when training camp opened, despite injuries to such key performers as quarterback Frank Ryan (who shoved back the pain and played anyway) and receivers Gary Collins and Milt Morin, the Browns won their division. They should win it again. Their offensive line remains one of the best around, and their defense has developed into a solid one. Coach Blanton Collier would—like most coaches—still like to have a more reliable pass rush, but the Browns' front four usually manage to do the job, and Cleveland's secondary is the best it's had in years.

The ST. LOUIS CARDINALS' hopes for this season lie upon the youthful shoulders of quarterback Jim Hart, who showed great potential but also his lack of experience when he replaced Charley Johnson in '67. It would be too much to expect a quarterback in only his second year as a regular to direct a title team, but it's not impossible. The Cardinals have everything else necessary to make a good run at the Browns. Both St. Louis lines are strong, their running game—led by the still improving Johnny Roland—receiving and defensive secondary all are excellent.

The PITTSBURGH STEELERS' long search for a solid quarterback may have ended last season. Hard-luck Bill Nelsen—who had looked ready to come on for a couple of years only to be sidelined by injuries—had lost his job to young Kent Nix, and was traded to Cleveland. Coach Bill Austin still isn't satisfied with his offensive line or his running attack, but feels both are improving. And the Steelers continue to have their traditionally rugged defense, particularly when Ben McGee is healthy and rushing the passer from his end position.

The NEW ORLEANS SAINTS matched the top winning record (three games) of other expansion teams last season, but like some others, they may fall back a bit in their second season. However, they have one of the finest young coaches in the league, Tom Fears, and he's building for the future. Which is why he traded quarterback Gary Cuozzo to the Vikings for two draft choices.

AMERICAN FOOTBALL LEAGUE

We missed both predictions in the AFL last season, but, undaunted, we try again in '68:

WESTERN DIVISION	EASTERN DIVISION
Oakland	New York
Kansas City	Buffalo
San Diego	Houston
Denver	Boston
Cincinnati	Miami

The OAKLAND RAIDERS led the AFL in six offensive and nine defensive categories last season. Included in the offensive stats were most touchdowns scored (58) and most points scored (468). Included in the defensive stats were fewest first downs allowed (182), lowest average yardage allowed per rush (3.2), lowest percentage of pass completions allowed (41.2) and most times tackling quarterbacks for losses (67 for 666 yards). Small wonder the Raiders lost only one AFL game last season.

And unlike the Chiefs of a year ago, this team isn't likely to come apart in defending its championship. Daryle Lamonica was the league's leading passer last season, and his second year in Oakland should be even better, particularly if the Raiders come up with a top receiver with speed. Tight end Billy Cannon and wide receivers Bill Miller and Fred Biletnikoff are competent, but none is a deep threat. The Raiders will have their best runner, Clem Daniels, back this season, teaming with the much improved Hewritt Dixon.

The team's offensive line is solid, and the defensive line—led by tackle Tom Keating—is excellent. The linebackers, Bill Laskey, Dan Conners and Gus Otto, are fast developing into the top group in the league. Coach Johnny Rauch has fine cornermen in Kent McCloughan and Willie Brown, but he had four interchangeable safeties last season—which means none of them was strong enough to win the job outright. He'll try to settle on two regulars this season.

The KANSAS CITY CHIEFS continue to have, in the opinion of most experts, the best man-to-man personnel in the AFL. Just look at the galaxy of stars—offensive halfback Mike Garrett, quarterback Len Dawson, flanker Otis Taylor, offensive tackle Jim Tyrer, guard Ed Budde, linebacker Bobby Bell, defensive tackles Buck Buchanan and Ernie Ladd, defensive end Jerry Mays, safetymen Bobby Hunt and Johnny Robinson. . . . The Chiefs did suffer a rash of injuries last season, but the thought persists in many minds that Kansas City still did not play up to its ability. For one reason or another, the best is not brought out in this team by those in charge. Of course, if Hank Stram can put it all together as he did in '66, the Chiefs will give the Raiders a heck of a battle for the Western championship in '68.

The SAN DIEGO CHARGERS surprised everyone while rebuilding last season, but we can't see them matching their 8-5-1 record in '68. Coach Sid Gillman got rid of most of his aging superstars and brought in youngsters he could mold into a unit that would play better "team" football. Two kids who particularly seem to have a fine future are running backs Dick Post and Brad Hubbert. And Gillman has two outstanding receivers in Lance Alworth when he's healthy, which he wasn't for much of 67, and Willie Frazier. However, we feel the Chargers are still a year or two away from becoming a strong contender again.

The DENVER BRONCOS have a long way to go before they can hope to contend. But Lou Saban, in his first year as coach-general manager, wasted no time in cleaning out the dead wood last season. He will see this season if the youngsters who showed promise can really come on as professional football players. Quarterback Steve Tensi, acquired during the '67 season, is the key to whatever success the Broncos can achieve this year.

The CINCINNATI BENGALS come into the AFL this season, which is good because it evens off the league to ten teams and brings Paul Brown back into football where he belongs. He made a smart move in selecting youth with potential over tired veterans among the players made available to him by the other teams. He also had a fine draft of college players, perhaps the best in the history of expansion teams. Now just give Brown a few years to build.

The NEW YORK JETS are our choice in the Eastern Division because they have the top quarterback in the Eastern Division, Joe Namath. And the team's number one draft choice, Lee White of Weber State, is a big, strong fullback in the style of Jim Nance. Matt Snell and Emerson Boozer will be back to help the running game, and coach Weeb Ewbank is going to try to get more speed into his offensive line, which will also help. Namath has three excellent receivers to work with in Don Maynard, George Sauer (who led the league in total catches last season) and tight end Pete Lammons. Ewbank drafted a couple of pass rushers who should improve New York's pressure on opposing quarterbacks, and his secondary (with the return of Cornell Gordon) and linebackers are capable. Another thing, probably the biggest thing, the Jets have going for them is that there is no dominant team in the East.

The BUFFALO BILLS will have all their injured back and hopefully a quarterback with a strong arm again (Jack Kemp was hampered with tendonitis last season). A healthy Art Powell alone can mean eight to ten additional touchdowns this season, which would get the Bills right back into the race. The defense is solid, despite the fact that it gave up a lot of yardage in '67. When a defense plays 60 to 70 percent of the time, it is very difficult for it not to slip on its own weariness.

The HOUSTON OILERS were magicians last season, but we don't see coach Wally Lemm working his same magic again. This is a team with too many holes—particularly at quarterback—to seem capable of winning another title. However, Hoyle Granger and Woody Campbell are fine runners and if Pete Beathard does develop in his first full season with the Oilers, they will be tough. The defense, featuring a lot of new faces and men at new positions last season, was playing very well toward the end of the schedule. Led by cornerback Miller Farr and linebacker George Webster, this unit will again be the team's strength.

The BOSTON PATRIOTS have a good deal of strengthening to do before they can again challenge for the title. But with a super runner like Jim Nance, a few key men could do the job. Coach Mike Holovak hopes halfback R.C. Gamble from South Carolina State will help open up things for Nance this season. Holovak also drafted to refurbish his defense, but a consistent quarterback could take a lot of pressure off this unit. Babe Parilli will have to come back or Don Trull will have to come up for the Patriots to improve markedly.

Coach George Wilson found himself an outstanding young quarterback for the MIAMI DOLPHINS last season. After John Stofa (now with Cincinnati) was hurt, Wilson was forced to play rookie Bob Griese, and a potential star was born. Griese completed 50.2 percent of 331 passes for 2005 yards and 15 touchdowns. He has a top receiver to work with in Jack Clancy (67 catches) and if Wilson can come up with some more help the Dolphins could begin to move.

MIKE GARRETT During an exhibition game between the Kansas City Chiefs and the Houston Oilers last year, Oiler rookie defensive tackle Willie Parker jumped offside and, apparently unable to halt his 295 pounds of momentum, smacked into quarterback Pete Beathard. Mike Garrett, the Chiefs' 5'9", 195-pound halfback, felt Parker should have tried a bit harder to avoid hitting Beathard. Garrett leaped out of his crouch and punched Parker right in the face mask. Parker then threw a punch at Garrett, which was not at all a wise thing to do.

Every Chief ball player on the field went after Parker. A very nice, if short-lived, gang fight ensued. Garrett carefully stepped aside and watched in fascination as all those huge bodies thrashed away at one another.

"Wasn't it spectacular though?" Mike said later. "I just lost my head for a second. Actually, ever since last year I try not to get into fights. I got into one with Willie Brown, the Oakland defensive back who was then playing with the Broncos. He beat the heck out of me and afterward I got fined $50. It just isn't worth $50 to get the heck beat out of you."

However, it was reassuring to Garrett to see all of his teammates rush to his aid. They had reason to, of course. As a rookie in '66, Garrett had been one of the prime reasons why the Chiefs earned the right to play in the first Super Bowl. Mike had rushed for a team-leading 801 yards and gained another 175 on pass receptions. The Chiefs wanted to make sure nothing happened to their best running back before the season even opened.

It had not been at all like the year before when Mike reported to the Chiefs. The Chiefs' veteran players rode him unmercifully from the day he reported, nicknaming him Elmer Fudd and taking shots at him—physically and verbally—every chance they got. Garrett had won the

Heisman Trophy at USC in '65 and the Chiefs had signed him to a five-year contract reportedly worth between $300,000 and $400,000. Veteran players who are making $15,000 per season or less tend to resent bonus players, particularly when the object of all that monetary affection happens to be a 5'9", 195-pound running back. You can count on the hairs of Yul Brynner's head the number of running backs that size who were starring in pro football in '66. So the veterans got on Garrett and stayed there until he threw them off.

Mike knew it was going to be bad the first day he ran onto the practice field. "I heard a fan sitting there say, 'They paid all that money for *him?*'" Garrett recalls. "Mind you, I was just running out on the field."

Teammates got on him about his big bonus and his small size. Garrett, who reported three weeks after playing in the College All-Star Game, was having enough trouble learning the Chiefs' system and learning to play pro ball without having the hazing added to his burdens. What he did was try that much harder, more determined than ever to make it, to show his teammates they were making a mistake. Finally, Mike began pressing, and kept making mistakes himself. "Darn," a veteran would say, "the prize rookie made another mistake."

And they took shots at him in scrimmages, getting in little extra blows, little twists, testing him. Garrett put a stop to that one day. "I lowered the boom on a safety one play," he says, "and then they pretty much left me alone."

Fortunately, through all his harassment, through all his troubles in camp and in exhibition games, Garrett never lost faith in himself. And neither did Kansas City head coach Hank Stram, who told him: "I know you can make it. Take your time. Stop fighting yourself."

In the Chiefs' opening game of the season, Mike was used on the special teams, returning punts and kickoffs, and he knew he was going to have to prove himself here if he was ever going to get a good shot at running from scrimmage. He promptly set a club record by running back a punt 79 yards for a touchdown. The next week he was splitting time at halfback with Bert Coan, a 6'4", 220-pounder, revealing his slithering, wriggling, quick-cutting style and low center of gravity that made him such an elusive runner to bring down. Before the end of the season he was the regular halfback. In fact, in the last game, against San Diego, Mike carried the ball 25 times from scrimmage and gained 161 yards. That gave him a season's total of 801 yards rushing, and only one other AFL player, Boston's Jim Nance, had more. Garrett was the runaway choice for the league's Rookie-of-the-Year award.

Last season, even though the Chiefs faltered badly when they were heavily favored to win their second successive championship, Mike Garrett showed the first year had not been a fluke. He rushed from scrimmage a fantastic 236 times, gained 1087 yards (third high in the league only to Jim Nance) and scored nine touchdowns. He also caught 46 passes for 261 yards and a touchdown.

His biggest day—and the biggest any runner had in the AFL last season—came against the New York Jets. He rushed for 192 yards in 23 carries. Of the 19 times the Chiefs handled the ball in the third period, Garrett carried 12 times. He was running so strongly and so well that quarterback Lenny Dawson just kept calling his number. "One time I carried three times in a row," Mike recalls. "I came back to the huddle really winded. So I looked at Dawson with a kind of 'Lenny, I'm tired' look—but he called me again."

Garrett isn't supposed to be rushing the ball 23 times in a game, though, if the truth be known. His average for the season of almost 17 carries per game is probably a little high for him. He just isn't physically big enough to take the punishment a pro runner takes. The linemen who hit him are five to ten inches taller and 50 to 100 pounds heavier, and they hurt. Despite the fact that coach Hank Stram says that "Mike has the torso of a 240-pound man; he has broad shoulders and a thick neck," blocking alone is punishment for him.

When he first reported to the Chiefs he had poor pro blocking techniques because, although he was an excellent blocker in college, he was used to cutting down opponents on the run. His quarterback at USC rolled out, and he did very little blocking head-on. In the pros, the running backs have to sit there in front of their quarterback on pass plays and pick up anybody who crashes through. When the crasher was a guy like 313-pound Ernie Ladd (now Garrett's teammate but initially still a member of the Houston Oilers), Garrett was often the guy who was picked up and thrown away. Mike had to learn to hit low and drive right through his opponent's legs or hips.

But Mike just doesn't have the size ever to be a great blocker. His ribs cannot take the pounding. John Bramlett, the heavy-handed (some say heavy-headed) linebacker, knocked out Garrett on a blitz during Mike's rookie season, smashing in his face mask and breaking his nose. Last season he hurt Garrett even worse, driving his helmet into Mike's thigh in a pileup and causing him excruciating pain. "It was the worst I've ever experienced," says Mike. "It was just a deep bruise of the hamstring muscle, but it hurt."

It is often a gutter fight down on that field, and the big men like to destroy the little men any way they can. Mike recalls an exhibition game against the Jets last year when, as he was being tackled, defensive end Verlon Biggs grabbed his lip and twisted it. "He tried to tear it off," Mike contends. "I said to him: 'What are you trying to do?' but he just gave me a hateful look and walked off. He knows and I know he is stronger than I am."

It's not surprising, considering his size and the beating he takes, that Garrett says he doesn't expect to play pro football more than five years. "I don't think I can last much longer than five years," he says. Then he adds, "I want to work at something else, and I might get tired of the game by then anyway. Playing football when you don't want to would be miserable."

Garrett doesn't mind the roughness of the game; he thinks it is all part of football, which he loves very much right now. He admits, "I like to humiliate my man by faking him, if I can. Then he gets even by hurting me, if he can." But Mike, who is from a broken home, who as a youngster had few material advantages and who could have gotten in trouble if he hadn't been such an outstanding athlete (he was such a good baseball player that when he graduated from USC he also received a $100,000 bonus offer from the Pittsburgh Pirates to sign a baseball contract), feels there is other, more important work for him to do eventually. He wants to start a school for deprived children. "I am interested in the early socialization of children. Deprived children. Any color, but they have to be deprived. I want to reach these kids and bring them into the mainstream of American life."

It may be an "Impossible Dream," one of Mike's favorite songs, but Mike Garrett has achieved other seemingly impossible dreams. One remembers Mike's early trouble in '66 and juxtaposes this with that scene in late '66 in the visitor's locker room in New York when Chief captain Jerry Mays stood on a bench by Mike Garrett. Mike's 96 yards rushing had helped Kansas City clinch the AFL title, and Mays handed him a football, saying, "The game ball goes to the little man they all said was too small to make it in pro football, but who has been a giant on our team."

LES JOSEPHSON
A surprising thing happened to Les Josephson about halfway through the 1967 National Football League season. The Los Angeles Rams, his employers, applied a lighted match to his contract and filled out a new one that increased his salary by some $10,000, putting him in the $25,000 class. This was a class few people ever expected Les Josephson to attain.

You see, Les Josephson played football at a high school that was so small it couldn't field an 11-man team; he played college football at a school so small that, even in this day in which girls' colleges with football teams are checked out by the pros, no pro scout found his way to Augustana in Sioux Falls, South Dakota; and he played pro football during the two preceeding years with the Rams like a man who might expect to find himself engaged in another profession at any moment.

But when Ram owner Dan Reeves awarded his 25-year-old halfback with a new contract midway through the season it was indeed well-deserved. The former captain of Los Angeles' special teams was at that point leading the Rams in yards gained rushing, in pass receiving, and toward a play-off with the Green Bay Packers for the Western Conference title. The latter, of course, was a position few people ever expected the Rams to attain in '67, and the performance of Les Josephson, or Josie, as his teammates call him, was no small reason for his team's sudden rise.

Ironically, only the winter before the Rams had thought so little of Josephson's ability that they had made a big trade for veteran Viking halfback Tommy Mason, even though his battered knees made his future somewhat doubtful. Josephson had shown so poorly in '66 that he'd been called on to carry the ball a mere 14 times, and the Rams were desperate for a solid halfback to go with fullback Dick Bass. Mason was coming off another knee operation, though, and Ram coach George Allen didn't want to push him or risk injuring him during the exhibition season. So Josephson got a lot of playing time in the exhibition games and it gave him a chance to show that the hard work he'd put in between seasons had not been in vain.

Feeling he hadn't been strong enough in previous seasons, Josie had lifted weights all winter and reported to camp carrying ten extra pounds of muscle. It hadn't lessened his speed at all. However, Ram executive Elroy (Crazy Legs) Hirsch advised Josie that there were two other areas in which he could most improve himself. Hirsch said Josie's hands were too tense when he went out for passes and that he should work on relaxing and letting the ball come into his body. He also told the young halfback that he should work on his agility as a ball carrier so that he could make quicker cuts. Josie stayed after practice every night and caught pass after pass to "loosen" his hands, and in between receiving sessions he ran through rope mazes and did other agility drills to develop more quickness.

By the time the exhibition season opened Les Josephson was a different football player than the fellow who'd wasted on the bench for two seasons. George Allen still remembers his first look at the new Josephson in a game against Cleveland. "In two punches from the Browns' 13-yard line," Allen says, "he put the ball into the end zone, moving both inside and outside a packed defense. He always had pretty good power, but he had to develop an instant reaction and sneaky moves—and he did."

At season's end Josephson had gained 800 yards on 178 rushes for a 4.5 average and had caught 37 passes for 400 yards. And he still managed to play on the Rams' special teams with the same verve and determination that led him to captain these units when he was a substitute runner. Josie would be on the field for a long offensive drive, perhaps even score the touchdown, then he would line up and block for the conversion attempt, then he would trot down the field and line up with the kickoff team, then he would dash down the field to tackle the kick returner before taking a rest. It reached the point last season when veteran Ram linebacker Maxie Baughan shook his head as Josie came off the field after seven successive minutes of hard football. Said Baughan: "Get him a peanut seller's jacket. Get him a license to drive the bus back to the hotel. Set up a souvenir stand for him on the sideline. This boy just ain't gonna be happy when he finds out there's only two ways you can make a living at this game—on offense or defense."

George Allen came over and told Josie: "I'd turn over the coaching to you, too, except I want to stick around and see what you'll try next."

Josie himself was so used to hard work that he couldn't understand what everyone was excited about. The blond-haired, pale-complexioned youngster grew up on a 240-acre grain-hog-soybean farm in Minneota (population 1297), Minnesota. His daily routine as a boy was to arise at 5 a.m., do chores, tramp through snow drifts to school, make his way back through the snow, work until dark and do his homework.

"I've visited his hometown," says Elroy Hirsch. "And it's a region where farmers struggle in blizzards to feed their families, nobody has very much and people pull together. They're as unspoiled a community as you'll find anywhere. Josie brings this to football and it makes him one of the outstanding team athletes I've seen, in any sport."

Josie was practically the entire team in high school when he played eight-man football. None of the big colleges went after him, but Bob Burns, who was then coaching at little Augustana, liked kids who could do a lot of things on a football field. You see, the Augustana squad consisted of 23 players. In 1963, his senior season, Josie rushed for 850 yards in the obscure North Central Conference, but nobody seemed to know about it or care.

"At Augustana, a big crowd for us was 3500," says Les, "counting kids and dogs. None of the pro teams drafted me. I guess they'd heard they'd need a dogsled and guide to get where I was and sort of lost interest."

Jim Malmquist, who took over as Augustana coach before Josie's senior season, went to the NCAA coaches' meetings in January, 1964, determined to sell the pros on giving Josephson a chance. "I begged coaches to hear my story," Jim says, "that we had a boy of great ability. Nobody listened."

Nevertheless, that spring the veteran San Francisco 49er scout Lynn (Pappy) Waldorf arrived in Sioux Falls and checked Josie's speed. Wearing football cleats and shorts Josie ran the 40-yard dash in 4.6 and 4.7 seconds. Waldorf reportedly told him: "Not ten big men in the NFL are that fast. We'll sign you as a free agent."

Josie was already married and a father, and he wanted to try pro football. But he couldn't sign. He was the star high-jumper on the Augustana track team, and signing a pro contract would make him ineligible. He felt he owed it to his school to compete. He did. Then he waited for the 49ers or any other pro team to get in touch with him. The Vikings did, but made no attempt to sign him. A few weeks later the Dallas Cowboys, who were signing every potential big back they could find, finally found Josie. They gave him a $2000 bonus and an $11,000 contract for his signature.

After a few weeks in the Cowboy camp Josie became so discouraged about his ability ever to play pro football that one day he abruptly turned in his playbook to assistant coach Ermal Allen. "Don't sell yourself short so soon," Allen told him. "You'll never forgive yourself if you quit without giving it your best shot."

So Josie gave it one more shot and regained his confidence in an exhibition scrimmage with the Orange County All-Stars at the Cowboys' Thousand Oaks, California, training camp. He broke loose for three long runs and impressed Ram scout Johnny Sanders, who was looking for a big young running back. A few days later when injuries forced the Cowboys to seek line help, they traded Josephson to the Rams for tackle Jim Boeke, a deal that proved mutually satisfactory to both teams.

The Rams, at that time off to one of their usually bad starts, had Josie in the regular backfield by the third game of '64. Josephson promptly scored a 53-yard touchdown that gave Los Angeles its first win over the Packers in four years. Two weeks later Josie gained 138 yards rushing against the Eagles, and finished his promising rookie season with 451 yards on the ground, plus 269 on pass catches.

But he'd like to forget the two years that followed. "I can't tell you what went wrong with me, but I played poorly," he says. "One explanation," says Ram quarterback Roman Gabriel, "is that he started worrying and apologizing for his mistakes. He blamed everything on himself when we lost ten games in '65. He gave me so much 'sorry about that' in the huddle I wanted to kick his butt. He just worried so much it hurt his play."

All that, of course, has changed now. "I've rarely been stunned by a player the way I've been stunned by the change in Josie from one season to the next," says coach George Allen. "No one ever improved so much so quickly. And I've never coached anyone who was so willing to take on jobs—any job—and thank you for the chance."

SONNY JURGENSEN

Murray Olderman, the sports editor of Newspaper Enterprise Association, was talking last season to a former NFL coach about the great quarterbacks in professional football. "We're only talking about two," said the expert, who cannot be named because he's still officially involved in the game. One, of course, was John Unitas of the Colts. The other?

Sonny Jurgensen of the Redskins. That could come as a shock to many people even though they are aware that

Jurgensen's always setting some passing record or other, but he also plays with a loser year after year, and great quarterbacks usually aren't associated with losers.

"If you had to pick the best passer in football right now," the ex-coach told Olderman, "it's Jurgensen—no contest. Remember, he doesn't have the team to go with him like John does. The outstanding quality about Jurgensen is that he utilizes the talent the Redskins have as well as anybody I've ever seen. If he were with a team like Dallas, it's hard to tell what he'd do. . . . The thing about Jurgensen is that he can throw the ball *between* people. Surround your receiver with a couple of guys, put a linebacker in the way, and Sonny'll still get the ball to him.

"Give me either of them—John or Sonny. They're the class of the league. Bart Starr can think with them, but he can't pass with them when it comes to delivering the big bomb."

Despite the fact that he was playing with calcium deposits in his right elbow, last season Sonny Jurgensen gave probably his finest all-round performance as a passer. He won his first NFL passing championship, finishing first in most touchdowns (31) and in lowest percentage of interceptions (3.1), second in highest percentage of completions (56.7) and seventh in average yards gained per pass (7.38). In addition, Jurgensen set all-time league records for most passes attempted in a season (508), most completions (288) and total yards gained (3747).

Small wonder that many pro football people are coming to the conclusion that Jurgensen may very well be the best quarterback in the game. Redskin coach Otto Graham, who is not a guy to say anything he doesn't honestly believe, has maintained for a couple of years that Jurgensen's the best. "I have said it before and I will repeat it as many times as anybody wants to hear," Otto repeated last season. "Unitas and Starr notwithstanding, there's not a quarterback in pro football I would trade Sonny for."

Last season, when asked which quarterback would he take if given the choice, Unitas or Jurgensen, Dallas coach Tom Landry initially picked Unitas, the winner. But then Landry admitted that he didn't feel Unitas could do with the Redskins what Jurgensen has done. "I don't believe anybody can do the job with Washington that Jurgensen has done," said Landry. "Sonny's the only guy I've seen since Norm Van Brocklin who was able to win with just a passing game alone. And I haven't seen anybody since Van Brocklin have a day against us like Jurgensen had last week."

In his first seven games as a Redskin playing against Dallas, Jurgensen had some fantastic days, three times passing for more than 300 yards and once passing for more than 400 yards. He also completed three touchdown passes in three of those games. In Jurgensen's eighth game against Dallas, which Landry referred to, Sonny hit on 23 of 33 passes for 265 yards and two touchdowns. An excellent set of statistics, but seemingly not more impressive than some of his other games.

You had to be there to appreciate what Landry meant. Because in that second '67 meeting with the Cowboys, Jurgensen was literally a perfect passer. Except for four balls he simply threw away to avoid losses, all of his passes could have been caught that day. "I thought we had a good rush against him," Cowboy tackle Bob Lilly said afterward. "But he just wouldn't let us catch him back there. How can you get to a guy who must get rid of the ball in two seconds?" The fact was that the Cowboys didn't get to Jurgensen at all. The Redskins won, 27-20.

The Cowboys didn't get to Jurgensen mainly because of his quick release, probably the quickest in football. He has had to develop a quick release to survive with the teams he's had protecting him. Since 1961, his first year as a regular quarterback, Jurgensen has played with exactly one winning team. That was the Eagles in '61, the same team that Norm Van Brocklin had won a championship with the year before. Jurgensen himself, despite his inexperience as a regular, came very close. He set several passing records and the Eagles finished with a 10-4 record, a half-game behind the New York Giants. But Sonny has never had the benefit of an outstanding running game behind him or an outstanding offensive line in front of him.

Yet he has survived year after year on his skills—particularly his ability to get rid of the ball quickly, before the rush can bring him down. In October, 1967, Jurgensen went out to Los Angeles and up against the toughest front four in football—Merlin Olsen, Deacon Jones, Lamar

Lundy and Roger Brown of the Rams. They are not only difficult to throw against because of their great ability to overpower blockers and get to a quarterback; they are so tall, ranging from 6'5" to 6'7", that even if they don't get all the way through to him, a quarterback simply can't throw over their outstretched arms. But Sonny Jurgensen threw around them, and threw quickly. Where most quarterbacks need three to four seconds to set up and pass, Jurgensen, by concentrating primarily on short passes, cut that normal time in half.

"Most of the time he released the ball in a second and a half or a second and three-quarters," Olsen said afterward. "Even in a dummy scrimmage, with no blocker in front of you, you can't get to a passer that soon. His receivers run the fastest eight-yard patterns in football. And a completion requires fantastic timing, but they've got it. This is the most accurate short-passing team we've played.

"Sonny forced us to honor his short game. Then three or four times he went deeper to score. I won't say he was lucky on the long ones, but twice he was fortunate to get the ball off. He couldn't have seen the receiver either time."

At least twice he couldn't see his receiver for the wall of flesh bearing down on him. And once he *was* lucky, releasing the pass and aiming for the spot where the receiver should be, but throwing short. Charley Taylor picked up on the underthrown ball soon enough to turn and come back to make a remarkable catch. He turned the play into an 86-yard touchdown. But it takes great skill and great timing to be able to throw and hit your receiver without seeing him. Jurgensen did it many times against the Rams. At least one of his three touchdown passes to his tight end, Jerry Smith, came on just such a throw.

Jurgensen had only one so-called "bad" day all season. That was when he completed only six of 18 passes against the St. Louis Cardinals, who not only put tremendous pressure on Sonny but did a fine job of covering his receivers. Even with Charley Taylor out of that game, Jurgensen still had Smith and Bobby Mitchell and a rookie with excellent potential named John Love to aim at. The only trouble was, when they would get open, the blocking would break down and Jurgensen would also be down. When the blocking held, the receivers just weren't breaking free.

"A lot of mistakes were made in that game," Sonny said a few weeks afterward. "I feel like this, though: If I get enough time to throw and the receivers get into the clear, I can ordinarily hit them."

That, friends, is the way it is with Sonny Jurgensen. He can hit them and he does when he's permitted to. This is why the Redskins had the numbers one, two and four leading receivers in the National Football League last season. They are all good ones, but as Jurgensen once said to Tommy McDonald when the little flanker told Sonny he'd make him a great quarterback . . . the receiver is nothing until the quarterback throws him the ball.

It's just unfortunate that the Redskins were such a poor football team in 1967, particularly the defense. Although he had no running game, Jurgensen still managed to put a ton of points on the scoreboard, and in many games brought the Redskins from behind to take the lead with less than two minutes left to play. But in most of those games the Redskin defense collapsed and the team lost just before the final gun.

Otto Graham said before the season started: "We'll rise and fall with Jurgensen. Sonny is just the greatest passer I've ever seen." That, he admitted, definitely included Otto Graham. "Sonny's got a great arm, stronger than I had, he's a better thrower than I was and he can call plays and recognize defenses better than I did." But Otto Graham was the winningest quarterback of all time, and hopefully someday he'll put together a team that Sonny Jurgensen can win with so that he'll get the recognition from the general public that he deserves.

LEROY KELLY For the first time in three seasons with the Cleveland Browns, Leroy Kelly got a chance to win a starting job in 1966—and he finished second in the NFL in rushing with 1141 yards gained (Gale Sayers of the Bears passed him for the title on the season's final day). Then, in the 1967 season, Leroy Kelly took a gamble, probably the biggest gamble a running back can take. He refused to sign a contract with the Cleveland Browns and played out his option.

He was gambling (1) that he wouldn't get hurt and (2) that he would have another great season and be able to negotiate what he felt was a fair contract with the Cleveland Browns or any other team that might seek his services. It was a gamble that took a great deal of guts and confidence. It is not easy for a running back, even a great one like Leroy Kelly, to have great seasons every year. Look at Gale Sayers in '67: he rushed for 880 yards, and people who saw him play know he had another excellent season. But the numbers he produced, his statistics, were not super stats, particularly compared to his other seasons. Leroy Kelly couldn't afford to produce those kind of numbers in '67, even though his team might have fallen off as badly as Sayers' Chicago Bears did.

Kelly never said exactly what salary he was asking in '67 or what the Browns were offering, but Hal Lebovitz, the astute sports editor of the Cleveland *Plain Dealer*, reported the figures, and you can be sure they were fairly accurate. Kelly earned about $20,000 in 1966 and was asking for about $40,000 in 1967. Browns owner Art Modell was offering a salary of $35,000. Kelly refused to accept less than he thought he was worth to the team, and played out his option at an automatic reduction in salary of ten percent. Which means he played for $18,000, or thereabouts, in 1967, or $17,000 less than he could have earned. As noted, you have to respect Kelly's guts and his pride.

Also his skill. You see, the Cleveland Browns did not have an outstanding football team last season, and they did have more than their share of costly injuries—to their quarterback, Frank Ryan; to their top receiver, Gary Collins; and to various of their linemen, the same men who open the holes for Leroy Kelly. However Leroy Kelly had an outstanding season anyway.

He led the league in rushing with 1205 yards. He also led in rushing attempts (235), average yards gained per rush (5.1) and touchdowns scored on the ground (11). Leroy scored two more on pass receptions (he caught 20 for 282 yards), his total of 13 placing him only one behind league leader Homer Jones, the Giant flanker.

Kelly did a very smart thing early in the season when he broke off, by mutual consent, contract negotiations with Art Modell. "Mr. Modell says we'll get together after the season ends," Kelly said at the time. "Right now I'm concentrating on playing football and winning."

In other words, he didn't want to worry about the contract while there was football to be played. Reporters asked him what city he would like to play in if he and Modell didn't get together and Kelly was forced to go to another team. "I haven't even thought about playing for another team," Leroy said. "I don't want to leave Cleveland and I'm sure Art doesn't want me to leave. It's strictly a financial problem."

In every city the Browns played in through the season, he was questioned about playing out his option. Leroy kept telling everyone the same thing: "It is personal and I'd rather not talk about it. I'm just concentrating on winning, and I'll worry about the other thing after the season is over."

When the season was over and the Browns had finished second to the Cowboys and were training in Miami for the Playoff Bowl against the Los Angeles Rams, Kelly did talk about his position. "Art could have had me for a reasonable amount before the season," Leroy said. "But then he made the statement that one year doesn't make a superstar. Well, now I feel I'm in a position to ask for what I want and get it. I don't want to leave Cleveland. I have a lot of friends there, but you can't worry about your friends when you're talking about your livelihood. But if I don't get the money I'm entitled to next year, I won't be in Cleveland."

Kelly found himself in an excellent situation. He wasn't drafted by an American Football League team when he graduated from Morgan State, and therefore he could negotiate with any AFL team after his option year expired on May 1, 1968. He could also negotiate with any NFL team that was interested in him. Kelly and Modell were scheduled to sit down and renew their contract talks after the Pro Bowl game in late January. Modell kept saying he didn't think they'd have any trouble getting together: "Leroy gambled and won."

Then, on January 8th, Sonny Werblin, owner of the New York Jets, said he would be "very interested" in Leroy Kelly if he became a free agent in May. "Anybody who runs a football club would have to be very interested in a ball player like Kelly," said Werblin. This statement had to please Kelly more than it did Modell. There were rumors that the new AFL team in Cincinnati, Paul Brown's Bengals, also would talk to Kelly at the proper time.

A reporter asked Kelly if he was concerned about being blackballed by other pro football teams, because owners might not wish to precipitate a mass of option playouts by their stars who could sign for larger salaries elsewhere. "I wish they would try it," said Kelly. "They'll have the biggest law suit they've ever had."

It didn't come to that. In February the Browns announced that Kelly had signed a four-year contract. No figures were announced, because they seldom are in pro football, but experts speculated that for Kelly to tie himself up for that long a period, he must have gotten precisely what he wanted—say around $70,000 per year. "I am very much relieved it's over," said Leroy, who admitted during the '67 season that his gamble had put a definite crimp in his wardrobe.

Leroy Kelly not only leads the league in rushing, he leads it in fashionable dressing, too. "It has made things tight for me," Leroy told Philadelphia writer Bill Shefski in December. I can't work any new suits into my budget. I haven't bought a new suit since I was home [his family lives in Philadelphia, where he grew up] and bought three. I have to treat myself soon."

He has earned the right to. He became an even better football player in '67 than he was in '66. Although he was a four-year man, he was only a sophomore as a regular. He carried only six times from scrimmage in '64, and only 13 times the following season, though he did lead the NFL in punt returning, running back 17 for 265 yards and two touchdowns. But then Jim Brown made his surprise retirement announcement as the Browns went to training camp in '66 and Leroy Kelly found regular employment.

Cleveland coach Blanton Collier said at the time: "I don't expect to replace Jim Brown. Runners such as he was come along once in a lifetime. But I do expect someone from this squad to make a name for himself."

Leroy Kelly is the name. But a running back doesn't learn everything he has to in one season. Midway through last year he said, "My blocking has improved tremendously. I really worked on it." Unlike Jim Brown, the 205-pound Kelly was given more blocking responsibility and accepted it. He particularly likes cutting a path for his running partner on the Browns, fullback Ernie Green, whose fine blocking has contributed so much to Kelly's success.

Another area in which Kelly improved in '67 was hitting the holes and making his cuts at the precise moment his lineman do their jobs. Many experts feel Kelly has the quickest start in football. He seems to be through the line almost before Frank Ryan can turn and hand him the ball.

"Timing is the most important thing between the backs and linemen," Kelly said late last season. "A back has to vary his speed according to the type of play. He has to run under control a lot of times, and he has to take off on other plays. I'm still picking it up."

After Kelly had run wild in Cleveland's 34-14 win over the Steelers in '67, Pittsburgh linebacker Any Russell allowed as how the Browns' speedster had gotten his timing down fairly well. "Kelly is the greatest runner in the league today," said Russell. "He never cuts the wrong way and he uses his blockers better than any runner I've ever faced. I don't put him in the class with Jim Brown.

Brown was Superman. For human beings, though, Kelly is the greatest."

He is certainly the greatest gambler in football. But, of course, it takes great skill to be a great gambler, and Leroy Kelly has that in abundance.

DARYLE LAMONICA When Daryle Lamonica, the quarterback for the American Football League champion Oakland Raiders, was growing up in Fresno, California, he came very close to becoming a professional baseball player. Three pitchers he played high school ball with—Jim Maloney, Dick Ellsworth and Wade Blasingame—all signed lovely bonus contracts and made the major leagues. Daryle, a strong-armed infielder with a lot of power at the plate, was offered a $50,000 bonus by the Chicago Cubs to sign a contract when he graduated from high school.

"I thought that was all the money in the world," recalls Lamonica, "and I was ready to jump at it. I grew up on a ranch and I know what work is. We had 20 acres of fruit, peaches and apricots, and I'd be out there picking from sunup to sundown. When I was in high school I was the foreman of the ranch. I made my gas money and loose change and paid my way through school. I probably complained more than most kids, but I just have great parents. They urged me, along with my counselors in school, to go to college and I listened to them. I can't have any regrets about passing up baseball. I'll always have some doubt in my mind. But in my heart I'll always think I could have made it as a baseball player."

Daryle Lamonica also thinks he can do—and do very well—anything he sets out to. And he just won't quit until he does it. Former Raider coach and current managing partner of the team characterizes Lamonica with one word: "Persistence, I think that's the word for Daryle Lamonica. If you take a concrete wall and you stick four nails in it and you assign four men to drive those nails all the way in, this is what would happen: One guy would quit the first day. Another the second. Another the next day. But five days later Daryle Lamonica would still be there, hammering that nail into that concrete wall until it was all the way in."

After he'd accepted a scholarship to Notre Dame and reported for his first football practice, Lamonica found himself one of 12 quarterback candidates. Daryle beat out all of them and went on to become Notre Dame's regular signal-caller for his three varsity seasons. It took a bit of persistence for him to keep battling back those three years, too, because Notre Dame football was nothing like it is today. The fighting Irish suffered losing seasons consistently in those days.

"I hated to lose," Daryle says. "It was the school of hard knocks for me. But it made me a better competitor. We kept our chins up, and never got complacent."

Although he wasn't a great college quarterback, Daryle kept working at it on his own. (He had to, because Joe Kuharich was the Notre Dame coach then and he has never developed a top quarterback.) By the end of his senior year Lamonica was good enough to be drafted by the Packers, even if it was on the 12th round. That was ten rounds earlier than the Buffalo Bills of the AFL drafted him. Since Green Bay didn't offer him a spectacular contract, Daryle accepted the $12,000 salary and $2000 bonus from Buffalo, figuring he'd have a better chance of advancing there. He wondered if he'd made the right decision when he reported to camp and discovered 12 other quarterbacks were on hand. It was like Notre Dame all over again. "I had some sleepless nights," Daryle recalls.

But he made the team as the lone backup man behind veteran Jack Kemp in 1963 and had a fair rookie year, completing 33 of 71 passes for 437 yards and three touchdowns. The following year he replaced Kemp seven times when he wasn't moving the team—and won all seven games as the Bills took the league championship. The following season was when Lamonica's disenchantment with Buffalo set in. He felt he had earned a shot at the number one job, but he didn't get it.

"I played less in 1965, and in 1966—even though Jack

had a lame arm that year—I played even less," Daryle says. In the spring of '66 the 6'2", 215-pound Lamonica finally went to Bills coach Joel Collier and said, "I want a maximum shot at the number one job or I want to be traded." Lamonica had said similar things to newspapermen in other years, but they hadn't paid off. Once again, his persistence worked. Collier told Daryle he'd get his shot in '67 . . . and three days later he was traded to Oakland along with end Glenn Bass for quarterback Tom Flores and end Art Powell.

Lamonica was so surprised when he heard the news he couldn't believe it. He was coming in from the hills with veteran Buffalo end Ernie Warlick, thrilled by the fact that he had shot a 35-pound bobcat on the run with his pistol. He went to show some friends the kill he had in tow, but they ignored it as they excitedly told him about the trade they'd heard over the radio.

"I thought it was a rib," Daryle says. "I finally called the newspaper in Fresno, and when I found out it was true, I named that bobcat 'Raider' on the spot. I've got his head mounted as a constant reminder of one of the greatest days of my life."

He would be playing near his home—and he would get "a maximum shot at the number one quarterback job." Lamonica took full advantage of that opportunity under the careful guidance of Raider coach Johnny Rauch, himself a former quarterback.

Daryle started slowly during the exhibition season as he tried to become acclimated to his new teammates, get his timing down with his receivers, learn how his backs liked their handoffs made. It is one of the most difficult jobs in the game for a quarterback to take over a new ball club, but by the time the season opened he was ready. So were the rest of the Raiders, who had nothing but good things to say about the new man in charge of their future.

And take charge Lamonica did, leading the Raiders to 13 wins in 14 regular-season games, plus a victory in the AFL championship game over the Houston Oilers. He completed 220 of 425 passes for 3288 yards and a league-leading 30 touchdowns for the season. Not surprisingly, he was voted the AFL's Most Valuable Player.

Perhaps his greatest test came on December 3 when the Raiders met the Chargers, who had also lost only one game, in San Diego with the Western Division title at stake. San Diego coach Sid Gillman devised a clever, complex defense that utilized all manner of shifts and blitzes and unusual pass coverages in an attempt to shake up Lamonica. It didn't stop Daryle from hitting his flanker, Fred Biletnikoff, with an early 18-yard touchdown. After the Chargers had tied the score, Lamonica marched his team to a field goal.

"Then," Houston *Post* columnist Mickey Herskowitz wrote in *Sport Magazine,* "came the crusher. The Raiders had the ball on their own 36, third down and less than a foot to go. Lamonica broke his team from the huddle, hunched over the center and barked the signals. At the snap halfback Pete Banaszak came charging into the line. Nine Chargers, as one, stiffened and moved in to stop Banaszak from making that foot. But Banaszak did not have the ball. Lamonica giveth, and taketh away. He dropped back, with Charger troglodytes bearing down on him, and quickly lobbed a pass to tight end Billy Cannon. Cannon had made a perfunctory block at the line and headed downfield. He was all alone. He gathered the ball like a sleeping baby in his arms and ran 64 yards for the touchdown. Lamonica went on to throw touchdown passes to Bill Miller and another to Cannon, completing 21 of 34 passes for 232 yards. But it was that great call and perfect throw to Cannon that did it for Oakland as the Raiders rolled to 41-21 victory."

You wonder now if perhaps Lamonica hadn't been right for a couple of years when he claimed he should be a regular quarterback. He wonders, too, in retrospect. "You hear some say it takes six years to make a pro quarterback," Daryle says. "Some say you need only as long as it takes to get the experience. As far as I'm concerned, I went through a learning process that all quarterbacks go through. I'm grateful I played under Lou Saban [his original coach with the Bills], who brought me along slow and didn't toss me into the fire. I was hard-headed at the time, but I'm grateful for it now. He developed me. It was a four-year education, and when I got the shot last year I was able to capitalize on it. I can't say it was wrong because it all fell into place for me. Now I'm playing for one of the great quarterback coaches in the business, John

Rauch. I've never gone into a game that I wasn't mentally ready for."

Rauch himself is frank to admit he had no idea Lamonica would come on so quickly with the Raiders. He is also frank to predict that Daryle's fine first season in Oakland was only for openers. Al Davis concurs, saying, "Daryle did a wonderful job for us, but he isn't as good as he's going to be two years from now."

As for Daryle, he simply says, "All I want is to be the best there is. I've had my ups and downs. I set my goals high, and I'm never satisfied until I get there."

Persistent people are like that.

DICK LeBEAU Dick LeBeau, the veteran cornerback for the Detroit Lions, was leaving his apartment on his way to practice when down the corridor he suddenly spotted an old lady with frizzled gray hair and stockings rolled around her ankles. LeBeau's eyes rolled about madly as he flattened himself against the wall and said to the guy with him: "That's the witch I told you about. I've heard her dancing around a caldron and mumbling incantations: 'Leg of a frog, eye of a fly, gizzard of a lizard.' "

Dick LeBeau's mind is alive with this kind of vision. "I am thinking of becoming a spiritualistic medium," he tells you, "because I seem to have a natural talent for that. I have recently discovered that I can bring back Ben Franklin if I can just hit E minor on my guitar. Ol' Ben really digs E minor."

It would surprise no one who knows Dick LeBeau well if he was in fact able to communicate with Ben Franklin. Most agree with Lion broadcaster and former assistant coach Sonny Grandelius, who says, "The most interesting thing about Dick is his mind. I think Dick LeBeau can do anything he puts his mind to."

Like one of his favorite heroes, Ben Franklin, LeBeau

puts his mind to just about everything. In addition to playing defense with Detroit for nine years—which he has done well enough to earn trips to the Pro Bowl in three of the last four seasons, and to rate among the NFL's top two cornerbacks last year according to a poll of NFL scouts by *Sport Magazine*—LeBeau is a Renaissance man. He writes music and song lyrics, poetry, fiction, historical outlines and is compiling his own thesaurus. He plays the guitar (self-taught), golf (75, 76), pool (defending champ of the Lions), cards (ask to be excused when he sits down at the table), and he sketches and paints (realistic watercolors).

"To me," he says, "anything I don't know about is interesting. I want to know everything I can grasp, collect all the knowledge I can. And I like to give creative things a shot. I enjoy gaping around museums. You see something and you say, 'I wonder what it's like to try to get that feeling, that effect in a painting . . .' It's fun just to see what you can do. The amazing thing is, if you just apply yourself, eventually you'll come up with something that's presentable."

Application is what has made Dick LeBeau such a fine football player. To him football is a full-time job and he refuses to accept any employment at all during the season. Every Thursday or Friday in season he spends hours studying films of Detroit's next opponent, of the receivers and quarterbacks he will face. "Films are a heckuvan aid to a cornerman," he says. "And anything you can do in preparation, you better do it, because you don't play football that long."

Dick is such a witty and imaginative guy that his intense involvement with football doesn't show except during workouts and just before ball games. Which is why he never looks at films or really bears down on his next opponent until late in the week. He simply can't sustain the emotional pressure for too long. Because any time he concentrates on his game plan, he projects right into the game itself. "If I start bearing down on Monday," he says, "by Sunday I may give it one of these numbers:" and he blinks his eyes spastically.

Laughter helps relieve the tension. "I think football is a game you become so emotionally involved in . . . well, if there isn't a bit of levity, you gotta lose track of what's happening. I've always been a great guy for relaxing, at the proper time."

LeBeau feels the emotional demands of playing his position are more harassing than the physical demands. "A cornerman has to kid himself into believing he's never gonna get beat," LeBeau says. "But if you keep your job long enough, somebody's gonna burn the spit out of you. When that happens you've got to kid yourself again. You've got to be able to come back ... or you have to quit."

There's no question about the fact that the cornerback has the toughest job in football. He stands back there all alone and trys to contend with the fastest, most agile people in the world. And no matter how good he is, how well he's prepared, at times other forces leap up to beat him. There was that play against the 49ers' Dave Parks in 1966, for example. Parks ran a little hitch pattern and LeBeau came up fast to cover him. When Dick reacted, Parks turned up field and LeBeau cut after him. But when he did so the field came apart beneath Dick's feet and he fell. All he could do was lie there and hope the rush got the quarterback. It didn't.

"That's the emptiest feeling in the world," Dick says. "That's why I always say you learn humility on the corner."

You also learn, if you are a good one like LeBeau, to make the big play. Consider the Lions' opening game of last season, against the Packers, who were favored by 14 points, in Green Bay. The Lion offense, which has been rebuilding ever since Bobby Layne was traded in 1958, managed to score ten points in the first half and the defense scored seven. But in the second half the Lion defense seemed to be on the field virtually every minute. What it finally came down to, with the Lions leading 17-14 and only three minutes left on the clock, was a great and gutty play by LeBeau.

With a third-and-19 from his three-yard line, Packer quarterback Bart Starr found his primary receivers covered and flipped a safety-valve pass to halfback Elijah Pitts. Faking cleverly, Pitts popped out of the crush of Lions on the right side and raced down the sideline. In seconds he was at the 50 and it appeared no Lion would get near him. Suddenly, from his position all the way across the field came LeBeau. Angling in, Dick didn't seem to gain a silly millimeter for 30 yards, and he couldn't have been expected to on the speedier Pitts. But somehow, pulling the hot air into his lungs on the 80-degree day and pulling out something from deep within him, LeBeau caught Pitts, jumping on his back at the 15 and dropping him at the 13.

It saved the ballgame, as the Packers were forced to settle for a field goal and a tie.

"I was so surprised when I caught up with him," LeBeau said in the locker room, "I didn't know if I was gonna get him down."

In the Packer clubhouse flanker Boyd Dowler and split end Carroll Dale both talked about how much they respected LeBeau's coverage of them (only one pass had been caught on him all afternoon, and Dick had come very close to his 33rd career interception on a sideline throw meant for Dale). "I feel cornerback is the most difficult position to play," said Dale. "It takes a really great athlete to perform well there. I know I couldn't do it. Dick's a good one."

"Dick's a hardnose," added the smiling Dowler. "He likes to come up and intimidate you."

"You turn your head on him and you're liable to find his elbow in your face," said Dale, who wasn't smiling. "It's nothing illegal, but I don't know whether it's necessary."

"I definitely do," Dick said later. "Let me stress that I've never intentionally made a dirty play in my life, because this is the way I like to live. But if you come near me and you're not in the pattern and I have a chance to hit you—I'm gonna hit you." He chuckled. "I think it's half of survival on the corner. You've got to make them conscious of you. Because if he can run his route unimpeded, go down there and set you up—he's gonna *kill* you."

Dick was killed a number of times during his first year as a Lion regular. But he has been beaten for touchdowns very seldom since then. An All-State quarterback at London (Ohio) High School, Dick took his 98.4 scholastic average to Ohio State on an athletic scholarship. After his freshman season he was switched from quarterback to halfback, playing both ways. His best season was as a junior when, though primarily a blocking back while on offense, he still rushed for 379 yards on State's '58 Rose Bowl team.

Although the 6'1", 185-pounder played defense, the experience did him little good after he was drafted by the Cleveland Browns in 1960. He had no background in man-to-man coverage, the pros' style, and was cut just before the season opened. He ended up on the Lions' taxi squad, and six weeks later he was activated and given a starting assignment at safety, where he did all right. The following year he and another youngster, Jim Steffen, won the starting cornerback jobs in training camp. Dick worked on the left side until the Lions traded for the NFL's all-time great left cornerman, Dick (Night Train) Lane. That day LeBeau went to coach George Wilson and said, "You know, George, I was a *right* cornerman all through college." Wilson tried him on the right side, and Dick's been there ever since.

Until Lane retired a few years ago, LeBeau was overshadowed by his super teammate. In fact, because opponents were afraid to throw at Lane's side, the newspapers tended to regard LeBeau as "the weak man in the Lion defense." It didn't bother Dick at all.

"I was perfectly content with my situation," Dick said last season, "because it's pretty good employment. But I began to feel in 1962—when we had probably the greatest defensive team I'll ever play on—that I must not be doing a bad job. A defense can't set records with a weak cornerman. And while I'm a better ball player today, because you do improve constantly, you never improve in the ratio that the pen improves you. But either you work on the weakest part of your game while maintaining your strength, or you go in the other direction and out. It takes assiduous application to maintain a level of performance, but even though it's trite and redundant, you've never gotten as good as you can be. There's no limit to a human's capacities to accomplish things."

Which is why the multi-talented Charles Richard Le-Beau will periodically sit at a restaurant table with his teammates, tilt his closed eyes upward and, rapping on the table two times, say, "If you can hear me, knock twice, Ben!"

One of these days Ben Franklin just may answer.

BOB LILLY Bob Lilly, the defensive tackle for the Dallas Cowboys who has made All-Pro the past four years, has come to expect opponents to break the rules. Lilly, you see, has been held by more guys than Elizabeth Taylor. He has gotten used to the opposition's tactics and has even come to accept the holding, within limits.

"I don't mind being held," he says, "but when they start tearing my jersey off my shoulder pads, it's bad."

Sometimes it gets so bad that the 6'5", 255-pounder actually gets angry and goes stomping around yelling at officials to enforce the rules. But that only happens when the opposition is moving against the defense and leading in the ball game, as in the game the Eagles won over the Cowboys last season. After that one Lilly allowed as how the holding really had gotten out of hand. However, then he added, "It's no excuse. That's part of the game as long as the refs don't call it. We've just got to overcome that."

Perhaps Lilly's attitude is a reflection of the fact that he's so used to overcoming large obstacles that one more doesn't faze him. It is automatic now that every time he steps on a football field he can expect at least two men to block him. He is just so strong and so agile that opponents know one human being cannot stop him. So two men are assigned to block Lilly on most plays. On the others three men block him, two lineman and one of the running backs. Even this doesn't always stop Lilly. Last season he was credited with 38 unassisted tackles and 42 others in which he was joined by one or more teammates.

Cowboy coach Tom Landry says, "There is not one man who can contain Bob Lilly." In 1964, the year he first developed into a top tackle, Lilly broke the first block applied to him *every single time*. And he's better today, despite the holding.

"I can understand it," Bob says, sympathizing with offensive linemen everywhere. "There are only two ways around a blocker. If he guesses wrong with you, he's got to do something or the quarterbacks wouldn't live long."

Lilly is big and strong and agile, amazingly agile for a man his size, and it is this latter asset which most helps him to beat two offensive lineman who have the advantage of knowing the snap count and where the play is going. Probably his best game last season was against the New Orleans Saints. Admittedly they are the league's newest expansion team and admittedly their offensive line was their weakest area. But what Lilly did against the Saints a football player shouldn't be able to do against a team of Playboy Bunnies.

"He was double-teamed 27 times and broke through 24 of those times," Landry said. "Actually, I've never seen him play better than he has in the last two games."

No doubt the fact that Bob Lilly keeps his cool in the face of the opposition's holding has a good deal to do with his consistent success. But this is not to imply that Bob Lilly cannot get so angry on a football field that the anger eventually will boil over into violence. There was that exhibition game against the San Francisco 49ers in 1967, for example, when Lilly decided enough was enough and retaliated. Bob's anger was not precipitated by holding but by a few raps in the jaw too many from 49er running back Gary Lewis. The next thing spectators were treated to was a fight between Lilly and Lewis, closely followed by a full-scale, both-teams-swinging-en-masse brawl.

"For about three plays before," Lilly told Dallas writer Steve Perkins after the game, "Lewis had been elbowing me in the face as the play ended. This time I went in and let him have some back with my elbow, and I got him a good one. He couldn't take it, so we started fighting."

Lewis, some 25 pounds heavier than Lilly, made a very smart move, grabbing Bob's face mask to keep Lilly off him. Seeing this, Dallas defensive end George Andrie rushed over to help his teammate. "Next thing," George recalled, "I am on the ground and people are punching me and kneeing me in the kidneys. I mean, there had to be ten guys on top of me. I didn't like it. I get claustrophobia in closed-in-places." He turned to Lilly. "Never again, buddy. I come over to help you and I end up the punching bag."

Lilly, who didn't see much humor in the affair, had to smile at this. He had much to smile about most of last season, though. He had another great season and the Cowboys won the Eastern Conference title for the second successive year.

However, while they were preparing to meet the Cleveland Browns for that title game, a terrible tragedy struck Bob Lilly and his pretty wife Kitsy. After checking on her other children, Bob Jr., Katherine and Christienne, ages four to two, on the morning of December 18, Kitsy went in to feed seven-week-old Carmen Elizabeth. She had died in her sleep of some mysterious illness.

Cowboy general manager Tex Schramm and assistant GM Al Ward rushed to the house when they heard the news. Bob Lilly was in a state of almost total shock. "I sit at the table with Bob, Katherine and Christienne every morning," Bob said.

Schramm, trying to find some words of comfort, said, "You haven't had a chance to get as close to the baby as you did to the others."

"You couldn't look at Bob too long," Ward said later. "It's a tough thing to see a big guy like that. We'd overstayed our time. We left pretty quickly."

Lilly told them he didn't know when he'd be back at practice, and Schramm told him not to worry about practice at a time like that. Bob stayed home with his family for two days, until the funeral—which every member of the Cowboys attended—was over. Then he rejoined his teammates at their Thursday morning workout. One thing Schramm remembers Bob saying was: "I'm sure I'll get over it, but right now I feel like going out and tearing up Frank Ryan and everybody else."

Not surprisingly, the Cowboys beat the Browns by a score of 52-14, as Cleveland quarterback Ryan found Lilly in his backfield almost as much as he found his own running backs.

The following week Dallas met and lost to the Packers in sub-zero temperatures. It was the second successive year in which the Cowboys played like a team that would upset the great Green Bay club, only to be frustrated again in the closing seconds.

It is a measure of the greatness of Bob Lilly that he rebounded from this disappointment just as he rebounded from the tragic death of his child. On the airplane back to Dallas, Lilly was already looking ahead to the '68 season. He stopped defensive line coach Ernie Stautner in the aisle and said: "What we need right away at the practice field is one of those rope sets like we had at training camp." The most agile defensive tackle in professional football was interested in improving his agility. And not in the following season or in the training camp period six months away, but right then. "We're also going to need some weight-work, especially in the arms and shoulders (the better to overpower blockers with)," he told Stautner. "George (Andrie) and I and Jethro (Pugh, Dallas' other defensive tackle) are going to be out there working with the weights and the ropes as soon as we get back. I can't say for Willie (Townes, the fourth member of the Cowboy front four). George and Jethro and me will be there. Probably Willie, too."

He paused a moment, then added: "We've got it going now. We have no dissension on this team, we're real close—and we've got the boys who want it."

Later the former Texas Christian University All-America admitted to Steve Perkins: "I'm not as unhappy as I would have been . . . if what happened last week hadn't happened." He was referring to his personal loss. "This defeat, it hurts, but now I'm a man. I grew up last week. I have a deeper look at everything, I guess."

For the first time, Lilly said, he felt like he was an old pro now, a seasoned veteran, and he was enjoying it. In particular he was enjoying working with, helping and watching the development of Dallas' young linemen like Pugh and Townes. He was also still learning himself, a process he felt might continue as long as he played the game. "The second-and-12's when they were running up the middle on us," Bob gave as an example. "Jethro and I got that worked out. We fix it in the huddle now which way each of us will go, so we won't leave the middle open. There's a hole there, but they'll have a hard time finding it."

That's even if they do hold, which they will, because there's just nothing else a human being or two or three can do when he's playing against Bob Lilly.

DON MAYNARD Don Maynard, the New York Jet
flanker who in his tenth year of professional football led the AFL in yards gained on receptions (1434) and was second in number of receptions (71),
is a guy who has always done things a little differently.

His determination to be different goes all the way back
to his high school days at Colorado City, Texas. When one
of the stars of the team broke his leg and was lost for the
season, none of the other players wanted to wear his
jersey. It was number 13. "I asked for it," Don recalls. "It
was a challenge."

He has been wearing it ever since, through good times
and bad, and the number seems to take on new signifi-
cance to him every year. He was married on December
13. His wife was born on September 13. His brother has
two sons who were born on the 13th. His father and sister
were born on the 13th. His parents now live in Odessa,
Texas, at 813 West 13th Street.

When Maynard, one of three original New York Titans
who are still with the team, joined the club in 1960 he
shared an apartment with halfback Billy Mathis, a Geor-
gian. "We were both a little strange in the city," Mathis
recalls. "We would walk down Times Square and look at
the buildings. I felt out of place with my Southern drawl.
Not him. He would put on his cowboy boots and blue
jeans and shine up his belt buckle and just talk his Texas
twang. He'd walk up to a newsstand, buy a paper and put
it down in this expense book he always carried to record
every penny he spends. He's a wonderful guy, but he's
sure different."

Don was wearing long sideburns way before they became popular. Now that many guys are wearing them,
Don keeps his cut short. But this doesn't mean he has
changed his desire to be different. Consider the all-
purpose cleaning fluid he distributes and sells called Swipe.

54

"It's non-toxic, non-flammable and does 300 different things," says Don. He was making this sales pitch to the Lions Club in Peekskill, New York, where the Jet training camp is located, before the '67 season opened. But the audience couldn't believe an all-purpose cleaner could be non-toxic. So Don drank some. "I went out and practiced later," Don says. "All it did was give me 'cotton mouth,' but it sure proved my point. You see, it does the job others claim to do."

Don Maynard does the job, too. Against the Oakland Raiders in December, 1967, he came up with the best performance of any receiver in the league last season. He caught 12 passes for 159 yards and two touchdowns. How does the 6'1", 180-pounder do it? "You have to keep the defensive backs guessing," he says.

Dolphin defensive back Jim Warren says, "You can't give Maynard an inch. I like to play him close and give him a good shot at the line of scrimmage every time. If you give him a chance, he'll go deep. You have to stay close to him."

Walt Michaels, the coach of the Jet defensive backfield, has tried to stop Maynard enough in practice to fully appreciate the skinny flanker. "I've played with a lot of great receivers, like Mac Speedie and Ray Renfro on the Browns," says Michaels. "The closest way to describe Maynard is to say he's a lot like Renfro. Renfro had more moves, but Maynard has a great change of pace. Both are exceptionally fast—a 4.5 time in the 40-yard dash.

"That and Maynard's change of pace are his biggest assets. Everybody knows this. When many guys come down the field fast, they're going all-out. But while they're going all-out, Maynard is only at three-quarter speed. When you think he's going all-out, that's when he turns it on. Fast, slow, fast, slow. Finally he makes his move. I tell the guys in our secondary to keep going all out and never believe him."

A few years ago the fans in Shea Stadium couldn't believe it when Maynard dropped a sure touchdown pass in a night game that would have beaten the Chargers. When he dropped another long touchdown pass the following Saturday night, the boos rained down on him and the rumors started that Maynard had bad hands.

Michaels says that's ridiculous, that Maynard has excellent hands. "How can anyone believe those stories?" says Walt. "Just look what he's done here."

What Maynard has done in eight seasons as a Jet is catch 434 passes for 7913 yards and 65 touchdowns, which is a fantastic record, ranking him right up there with the top receivers in pro football.

Nevertheless, after Maynard dropped those two touchdown passes there were rumors he would be benched. He wasn't concerned, because he knows what he can do and doesn't feel the misses were really his fault. "There are 80 yards of lights at Shea," Don explained. "The ball was coming down in darkness and I had to guess where it was. just as it reached me, it came into the lights and went off my fingers. It looked bad. People started booing. My wife couldn't take it and went home. She never saw the second one, which happened the same way."

Jet coach Weeb Ewbank stuck with Maynard, though, and he came back and had a big game the next week. "I knew what happened and the Man upstairs knew," Don says now. "I told my wife to forget what all the people thought. I told her I'd be back in there the next week. Heck, if Mickey Mantle strikes out, he comes back the next day."

Maynard has always been able to come back. After starring in football and track in high school, Don received a scholarship in these sports to Rice, but he quit after one semester. He didn't dig Rice and he didn't dig being that far from home. In February he enrolled at Texas Western without a scholarship, but immediately won one as a sophomore halfback when he made the All-Conference team. "In my senior year, we beat every other team in our conference. That was the first time it was ever done."

He got married during that season and in doing so lost his athletic scholarship, but he didn't mind. He took a job in the cafeteria and his wife Marilyn went to work, too. Don graduated and subsequently earned his master's degree (he's a teacher in the off-season in addition to selling Swipe).

Don had already been drafted as a future choice by the Giants in 1957, and he made the team in '58 as a substitute running back and regular kick returner. He made the team despite his sideburns, which the Giant Coach at the time, Jim Lee Howell, ordered him to shave off.

"Yes, sir," said Don, who went to his room and painted number 13 on all his equipment, but decided not to shorten his sideburns.

"I thought I told you to shave those sideburns off," Howell said to him the next day.

"Yes, sir, you did," said Don.

"Why didn't you do it?"

"I like them."

He was still wearing them when he played in the NFL Eastern Conference playoff game in December of 1958. Maynard dropped a Cleveland punt, and even though the Giants won, 10-0, he wasn't long for the team. The following season he was cut and went to Canada for a year. "I signed a contract without an option because I wanted to be free when the American Football League got started," Don says.

He wrote to the Titans because he knew Sammy Baugh, who was coaching the team, would remember his performances against Abilene-Christian, which Baugh had coached when Don was in college. Sammy told Don to come on up. The Titans, you'll recall, ran a pretty loose operation. Their idea of pass patterns was "everybody go long." Don did very well under this system, catching 72 passes his first season, but it was not a good training ground, did not give him much discipline.

Which is why subsequent Titan and Jet quarterbacks complained about Maynard's breaking patterns. This, of course, caused considerable interceptions, the quarterback throwing to one spot and Don turning to another. When Weeb Ewbank took over the Jets, Maynard drove him crazy with his antics the first season. "Maynard could be a great receiver," Weeb would say, "all he has to do is follow the plays as they are written."

"I don't worry so much about that," Don would say. "All I want to do is get free. It's my job to get free and it's the quarterback's job to find me."

When Dick Wood was the Jet quarterback and was asked to run down Maynard's skills, Dick would say, "Maynard is fast."

All that has changed in recent years, though. "If Don breaks a pattern now," says Jet offense coach Clive Rush, "it's for a reason. I'm on the phone upstairs during the games now, and when Don comes off the field he communicates well. He reads coverages and constantly informs us of ways to beat the defense. He has tremendous concentration on the football in flight, regardless of what is happening around him on the field. He catches the long ball better than most people because of this."

Don Maynard also drinks more Swipe than most people because he is still different, too.

JOE NAMATH If there is one thing that stands out about Joe Namath and sets him apart from the crowd it is his courage. More than the fact that he received a $400,000 contract to perform the one job he wanted to do most, more than the fact that he lives in a penthouse with a llama rug and drives a gold Cadillac and goes out with girls, lots of girls, and parties and stays out later than most football players can afford to and wears his hair long and says what he thinks, does pretty much what he wants to at all times, and has developed into a top professional quarterback faster than anyone since Johnny Unitas. . . .

But you add all of these things up and, as unusual as they are, they are nothing compared to his courage. Consider his performance against the Raiders in Oakland late last season. The Jets were the only team to beat the Raiders in '67, having won early in New York. The Raiders were determined to stop the Jets this time, which meant stopping Joe Namath. So they mounted a furious pass rush, crashing in on Namath and flailing away at him every time he passed. As it turned out, they tackled him with the football only once all afternoon, but they hit him just as he was releasing the ball time and again, battering him to the ground, and they tackled him at least once after he released the ball. Defensive ends Ike Lassiter and Ben Davidson clobbered Namath on this play and Joe's helmet flew up in the air and Davidson's forearm smashed his face, cracking the Jet quarterback's cheekbone and fracturing his sinus. They helped him off the field and he didn't return to action. If the Jets had still been in the ball game, no doubt he would have. But despite Namath's 370 yards and three touchdowns gained passing with most of the fourth quarter still to play, the Jets were out of the game.

When Jet physician Dr. James Nicholas examined him, noted the swift swelling and suspected the fracture, Namath said, "I don't care what it is. I'm playing next week."

In the locker room writers found Joe trying to shave the right side of his jaw, which was twice as big as the left side. "I didn't take no beating," he responded to a questioner. "I got this at breakfast when I bit into a steak bone." Then he smiled. "What can I say? That's what this game's all about—hitting. If you can't take it, don't play."

"He's an athlete," said Dr. Nicholas, "a kid from the hard-knocks school. A football player either has courage in high school and college or he doesn't have it. There is no thought of courage now. It's instinctive to Namath."

It should be, after all the pain and surgery he has accepted to play football. He came out of the University of Alabama with a right knee that required delicate knee surgery and, subsequently, that he wear a cumbersome brace on it for support. Unconsciously he favored his damaged knee and strained the left one. Painful tendonitis set in the good one. Yet he kept playing, limping around in the backfield on what Jet guard Sam DeLuca (who himself was sidelined last season with a knee injury) described as "the worst knees I've ever seen."

He completed passes on those knees, unable to move about and escape any rushing linemen who broke through, but still getting off those passes by virtue of his amazing quick release and strong arm.

Flanker Don Maynard recalls catching a 55-yard touchdown pass from Namath in '66 when there seemed to be no way Joe could unload the ball before being hit. Two Houston Oiler lineman were right on top of Namath when Maynard made his cut. "We looked at the movies the next day, and you wouldn't believe it," Don says. "Those two guys smacked into Joe and ate him up. You could see Joe's elbow actually resting on one guy's shoulder as he threw."

"Psychologically it was a feat for him to go out there with those old-man's knees," DeLuca says. "It's tough enough out there when you can go 100 percent. When you can go only 50 percent, you got to be thinking: 'How will I do? Will I get hurt because I can't go all-out?' It has to affect you. But I'll say this for Joe and I admire him for it: Not once did I ever hear him complain about the pain or use the knees as a crutch when he had a bad day."

Namath completed 232 passes for 3379 yards in 1966, both league-leading tatals. But by the end of the season it was obvious he would need another operation on his right knee. It was giving way under him when he merely walked about. "It was awful to see him limping around out there, his knee swelling, having to be drained constantly," says Dr. Nicholas. "But the operation was not an elective. If the surgery failed, Joe Namath was through as a football player."

Joe told him to get on with it, and during the winter Dr. Nicholas took more cartilage out of the knee and transferred a tendon to give the joint more support. The operation was a complete success. Joe worked slowly to strengthen the knee, and by the time camp opened he was running almost as well as he had in college. In fact, Namath looked so mobile that Jet coach Weeb Ewbank inserted a few roll-out passes into the playbook. Namath called one, too, and scored a touchdown on the surprised Raiders in that losing game on the West Coast, rolling right and going into the corner of the end zone untouched. But that loss all but knocked the Jets out of contention for the Eastern Division title after they'd led in the race most of the way. Once Namath lost speedy halfback Emerson Boozer (he'd lost regular fullback Matt Snell early in the season), the Jets couldn't run wide and this really cramped Namath's play selection. Without a real running threat, he became a full-time passer; that is, a guy who had to throw on almost every play. And the defensive lines fired in on him all the more recklessly.

Nevertheless, Joe Namath made startling strides in his third season as a professional quarterback. Weeb Ewbank saw the difference in Namath at the end of the exhibition season. "Joe's a far better passer than he was the last two years," said the Jet coach. "We keep a record of every pass thrown in our practices. For the last two years Jim

Turner has had the best completion record. This year Joe's the leader."

Namath himself felt the second knee operation was the big reason for his success. "Yeah, I probably am completing passes I couldn't have completed last year. I feel better out there and I have better balance."

"He's also more experienced," added Ewbank. "He didn't misread a defense in the pre-season games."

He didn't misread many during the season, either. He completed 52.5 percent of his passes (a league-leading total of 258) for an all-time pro record of 4007 yards and 26 touchdowns. Namath had the best day of his career against Miami in October, passing for 415 yards.

"He's like a machine when he gets going," Bronco coach Lou Saban said afterward. "You've got to give him credit—he's a heck of a quarterback. He drives his team out on that field. He's tough, and he keeps 'em in there all the time."

Roger Leclerc, the Chicago Bear veteran who became Denver's middle linebacker in this game, was asked to rate Namath with the top quarterbacks in the National Football League. "Well, I guess he's closest to John Unitas. Namath really threaded needles out there today just like Unitas does for the Colts. It's the sign of a good quarterback when he can throw that quick one out there and complete it consistently. It makes the defensive backs play up tight, and then he can throw deep.

"I think Namath is a better deep thrower than Bart Starr and he completes the quick one like Unitas. And he recognizes the defenses the way both of them do. Of course, I can only rate Namath on his play this one day. If he can do this steadily . . . You have to wait and see. Starr and Unitas can do it game after game."

Namath doesn't have their consistency yet, and could hardly be expected to in only three years and playing with a team that has several holes to fill before it can be consistent. In the second game against Denver Namath played poorly, and he was almost as bad the following week against the Kansas City Chiefs.

"I've just been ridiculous the last couple of weeks," Namath admitted last December. "Against Denver I overthrew a couple of passes and they were intercepted. And last Sunday it was just plain stupidity on my part when

Freddy Williamson of Kansas City grabbed that one and went 77 yards for a touchdown. It was a bad choice on my part. I shouldn't have thrown the ball at all."

This is pretty unusal talk from a quarterback, or any other star athlete—to admit how poorly he's played. But writers have come to accept the fact that when they ask Joe Namath a question they will get an honest answer. Just as they have come to accept his courage on a football field.

JIM NANCE In his second year in the American Football League, fullback Jim Nance of the Boston Patriots rushed for more yardage than any other back in football: 1458 yards. When he reported to the Patriot training camp in 1967, Nance said, "Jimmy Brown's all-time one-season rushing record is 1863 yards, and I plan to get that record eventually. This is only my third year in pro football. I don't think I'll get it this year, but someday I will. Last year I wanted to be the best back in the league, and my goal this year is the same."

A couple of weeks later the Patriots played their first exhibition game against a National Football League team, the Baltimore Colts. Nance had been back with the team for only 24 hours, after attending National Guard training for two weeks, when the game began. The Colts rolled over the Patriots, 33-3, but they didn't roll over Jim Nance. The 240-pound fullback ran through the fiery Baltimore line 15 times and picked up 64 yards, an average of 4.3 yards per rush. Considering his lack of practice for two weeks and the fact that the Colts jumped ahead and the Patriots had to play catch-up football, Nance was not at all disappointed in his personal performance.

But then, he had always been supremely confident in his ability to do the job through the Patriot line and under the offense devised by head coach Mike Holovak. "They can't stop me going up the middle with our system," Jim said in the locker room after the game. "No matter what they do to defense us, they can't stop me from finding a hole. With our system of optional blocking, optional running, there are so many things I can do when I got up the middle. If there's a hole where it's supposed to be, I take it. If there's not, I find my own hole. It's a split-decision thing; I can't delay. But I take a little turn here, a little turn there, and I'm off."

However, when the season opened, Nance did not get off and running. In the first two games of the season, against the Denver Broncos and San Diego Chargers, neither of whom was supposed to have outstanding defenses, Nance ran from scrimmage 33 times and gained only 114 yards, an average of 3.5 yards per carry. The lone touchdown he scored came on a pass reception.

After the San Diego game, Charger middle linebacker Rick Redman commented, "Nance still runs as hard and hits as hard, but some of his moves are getting stereotyped. It seems he always cuts back towards the middle, hoping to catch the linebacker going in the wrong direction. And, of course, all his plays are still right up the middle, too."

"We like to run Jim from tackle to tackle," said Mike Holovak, "because this is where he runs best. From the way teams are playing us now, it looks like they're setting their defenses to stop him inside. So we're just going to have to run him outside and force them out of packing the middle against him."

Holovak was shocked when he found that Nance's longest run in the first two games was for only seven yards. "When Jim carries 33 times, I expect him to break for 20 yards at least a couple of times," Mike said. "When he does that, it means we're at least getting into field goal position a number of times. In the two games so far we've tried only one field goal. For us that's unheard of (with a placekicker like Gino Cappelletti on hand). That shows how few opportunities we're creating for ourselves."

That was the real problem. The Patriot team wasn't creating opportunities for itself because it wasn't able to. You see, the Patriots were one of the weakest teams in the league last year. They slipped from a solid challenge for the Eastern Division title in '66 to next-to-last place in '67. The once-proud defensive unit had trouble stopping anyone, the team would fall behind, and quarterback Babe Parilli would have to start passing play after play to try to get back in the game, rather than going with the balanced offense of the game plan.

Nance didn't get discouraged, though. He still had confidence in himself and his teammates. "I just need to bust for one long gainer and things will get back to normal," he said when the season was still young. "That first one is important, because it gets the opponents thinking. Would you believe I haven't gotten as far as the safetyman once yet? That was my forte last season— crushing through and zinging that safety, getting him and his teammates thinking.

"But opponents are pinching in against me this year, bunching the middle. I'll have to start going outside more. Another thing you'll probably see are some draw plays and screen passes to me. We haven't run either this season. In fact, we only used five or six draws and one screen to me all last season. We had them in our repertoire, but rarely needed them. Now may be the time."

The variety didn't help that much. Jim Nance remained essentially a hard-driving fullback whose forte was banging up the middle, getting his yardage the toughest way. There's no question but if the Patriots had had a speedy halfback who was a threat to the outside it would have opened up the middle and taken some of the pressure off Nance. But the Pats had no such ballplayer. So week after week Nance did his thing to the best of his ability.

In doing so, he took a terrible physical beating. Even his teammates didn't know how Jim held up under the pounding. "You can really see those other guys looking for him," said Larry Eisenhower, the big, tough, veteran defensive end for the Patriots. "It seems like they all want a piece of him. Some of the shots he's taken this year are unbelievable. They hit him so hard he just shakes all over. Still, he gets up. I don't know what we pay him, but whatever it is he earns every penny of it."

During his first two years in the league, Nance would be sore after ball games for one or two days, no more. After the Patriots' first game last season against the expansion Miami Dolphins, Boston *Globe* writer Will McDonough found Nance still aching on Thursday. "I took a tremendous beating," Jim admitted. "Monday and Tuesday I

Mike Garrett, Kansas City Chiefs

Les Josephson, Los Angeles Rams

Sonny Jurgensen, Washington Redskins

Leroy Kelly, Cleveland Browns *(Photo: UPI)*

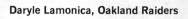

Daryle Lamonica, Oakland Raiders

Dick LeBeau, Detroit Lions

Bob Lilly, Dallas Cowboys

Don Maynard, New York Jets

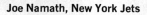

Joe Namath, New York Jets

Jim Nance, Boston Patriots

Willie Richardson, Baltimore Colts *(Photo: UPI)*

Dave Robinson, Green Bay Packers

Bart Starr, Green Bay Packers

Gale Sayers, Chicago Bears *(Photo: UPI)*

Charley Taylor, Washington Redskins

Johnny Unitas, Baltimore Colts

could hardly move. I wanted to go down to my lounge (a go-go club he owns in Boston) to do some work but I stayed home instead. Wednesday I planned to go to a movie, but I fell asleep in front of the television, I was so tired."

Not only were the defenses taking their toll by stacking against him, they were punishing him when he was blocking in the backfield. "Last year when I was blocking," Jim said, "the man I was supposed to block would try to avoid me. This year they're coming full speed and trying to hit me as hard as they can. Sometimes you get hit just as hard when you're blocking as when you're running."

The battering reached the point where some people wondered how much Nance could take. "He gets hit so hard that sometimes I flinch on the sidelines," said Patriot trainer Bill Bates. "Everyone has a different level of tolerance when it comes to pain. Some players can't stand any pain at all. Others can endure almost anything—and Nance is at the top of that category."

Nance himself kept saying he wanted to carry the ball "25 or more times a game. Before I'm finished in this game there are a lot of records I'd like to put out of sight. To set records, you've got to carry the football a lot."

"A guy has to love the challenge he faces in each game to respond like Nance does," said Larry Eisenhower. "He has to or he would have been whipped a long time ago. But no one whips Nance. He takes everything they have to offer and comes back."

Toward the end of the season Nance was not carrying as often. In one two-game stretch in November he carried only 20 times, which he feels should be his minimum for one game. The offense was built around him, but the offense simply wasn't functioning. "The most frustrating thing about this whole year is that I can't do anything about it," Jim said. "I just have to keep running in there and trying to make as many yards as I can according to the way that particular play is designed. When you're losing like this you're not the same player. On a winning team you can take chances. Once in a while you can gamble on a certain move, hoping it will take you all the way. With the way we're going, though, I don't take chances.

"This season has been one long lesson to me. I learned what it's like to be keyed on constantly—to be a marked man."

At season's end it was learned that Nance had been playing in intense pain every time he hit or was hit on his left shoulder. He has a slight separation there as a result of the pounding he took in rushing for a record 208 yards in a game against Oakland in '66. Doctors ruled out the possibility of an operation to repair the shoulder, fearing more harm than good might be done.

Nevertheless, with all the problems Jim Nance faced in '67, he was still voted the Patriots' Most Valuable Player. More important, he also gained more yards rushing (1216, averaging 4.5 per carry) than any other back in either league last season. Which is truly fantastic, considering.

WILLIE RICHARDSON

It was the Colts vs. the Packers, and as usual the Colts could not afford to lose the ball game. Locked in a tight race with the Los Angeles Rams and the San Francisco 49ers in the Coastal Division of the National Football League, the Baltimore players knew that if they were going to avoid the frustration they had known for the last two years— frustration caused by these same Packers—they had to beat Green Bay in this the lone regular-season meeting between the two teams.

Colt flanker Willie Richardson knew that if his team was going to win, he was going to have to start doing something. With less than seven minutes left to play, the Colts trailed 10-0 and Richardson hadn't caught a football since the pre-game warmups ended. Then Willie caught a pass for a first down and the team began to move. Colt quarterback John Unitas hit another first down, then looked to Richardson again. The ball was tipped by an onrushing lineman just as Unitas threw. But Willie saw that his quarterback was in trouble and uncovered, breaking his pattern, whirling and running back toward the line. He leaped and caught the ball for a 15-yard gain. In seconds Unitas hit Alex Hawkins for a touchdown. The PAT was blocked, but the Colts tried an on-side kick and recovered the ball on the Packer 34.

There was a minute and 34 seconds on the clock. In four plays the Colts gained 11 yards and a first down. And then Willie Richardson—who had spent most of his first four seasons as a Colt on the bench because he hadn't shown enough maturity to warrant regular status despite his physical skills—arrived as a professional. As the Colts huddled around center Dick Syzmanski, Willie Richardson leaned in and told Unitas: "I can beat Adderley to the inside."

Adderley is Herb Adderley, the Packer cornerback who had done such a good job on Richardson most of the game. But injured Colt receiver Raymond Berry had noticed from the bench that Adderley had been shading Richardson to the outside. Raymond told Willie a good outside fake on a post pattern should get him open.

It did. Not wide open, because Adderley recovered enough to jump and tip the pass—but open enough for Willie himself to go up and come down with the ball in the end zone. Willie promptly turned and threw the ball high into the Baltimore Memorial Stadium stands, shrieking with joy. That play epitomized his arrival as a Colt. Willie Richardson went on to catch a total of 63 passes last season, finishing third in the NFL, good for 860 yards and eight touchdowns.

But there was another play in another game in 1964 that stands out with equal prominence in Willie Richardson's mind. It is a play he does not enjoy remembering, but it epitomizes his problems as a pro up to the 1967 season. The play occurred in the fourth quarter of a game against the Minnesota Vikings. Richardson, normally a reserve flanker, was filling in at split end for the sidelined Berry. The Colts were behind by three points and it was third and ten for a first down when Unitas called for Willie to run a pattern over the middle.

"It was a critical situation," Richardson told writer Doug Brown last season. "I ran down and in and got open, but John couldn't get the ball off. He had to run out of the pocket. Instead of turning and running toward the sideline in the direction he was going—to make it easier for him to throw to me—I kept going toward the middle. It was a difficult throw for him and he couldn't hit me."

The Colts had to give up the ball, and as Unitas walked off the field he chewed out Willie with appropriate hand motions for all the stands to see. Richardson didn't even hear what his quarterback said, except that he had run the wrong way. He walked to the sideline with his head down, the shame burning inside him. Coach Don Shula kept him on the sideline, too, sending in Hawkins, who minutes later caught the winning touchdown pass.

Coach Don Shula told the press afterwards that inexperience caused Willie's costly error and explained that the game was so close he felt he had to replace Richardson with the experienced Hawkins. At about that time Unitas came by the cubicle where the dejected Richardson sat. "You'll be okay," John told him. "You'll work it out. Don't worry about it."

But it wasn't until last season that Richardson did. After being drafted on the seventh round by the Colts in '63, Willie started off well enough. He couldn't beat out veteran flanker Jimmy Orr for a regular job, but when Orr was injured Willie filled in for him and caught 17 passes for 204 yards as a rookie. In '64, the year of his costly-mistake, Willie caught one pass. In '65 Orr had his greatest season in a long and illustrious career; Richardson caught one pass.

"I was really disgusted," Willie recalls. "I thought I should be playing. After the fourth or fifth game, I was really down and went to Shula. He told me Orr was doing a good job, but I wasn't satisfied." So he went to team-owner Carroll Rosenbloom, who told him to take it easy, he'd get his chance. "You'll be a good one. It's just a matter of time."

The following year Willie arrived at training camp determined to excel. He did in the exhibition games, but again Orr was the regular when the season opened and caught 37 passes before an injury sidelined him. Willie filled in well, catching 14 passes for 246 yards and two touchdowns, but it was apparent that Unitas still didn't have a lot of confidence in him.

It wasn't that John didn't like Richardson personally,

because they communicated very well on a golf course or over a pool table or just sitting around having a few beers.

What was the problem on the field? Well, at Jackson State College in Mississippi, Willie Richardson was a legend in his time. As a sophomore he set an NAIA record by going 1227 yards on passes caught; then he got better. "He was *all* of Jackson State," says Buddy Young, the former Colt official who is now an assistant to NFL Commissioner Pete Rozelle. "He thought what he did at Jackson State he could do as a pro."

He couldn't, the pro game is too precise, calls for too much discipline from every player. "When he did get the chance to prove himself," says Shula, "he didn't produce. There were times when even the coaching staff and the other players were down on him.'"

"A lot of times Willie would run poor patterns," Unitas recalled last season. "It was a question of him making up his mind to run them right. That day against the Vikings [in '64] when I got angry, I had already thrown when he started to move the other way. I'm expected to do the right thing and I've got to expect my receivers to do the right thing, too. The thing is, a receiver has to reach the point where he does the right thing automatically."

In the second game of the 1967 season Willie Richardson, in his fifth year in the league, did just that. Orr had been sidelined in the opening game and the 6'2", 198-pound Richardson was now the Colts' regular flanker, for better or for worse. And Willie couldn't have been much better in this game against the Eagles. He caught 11 passes for 184 yards and two touchdowns.

In the raucous Baltimore locker room, Richardson experienced the unique, for him, excitement of being surrounded by reporters and bombarded by kidding remarks from teammates. "Give me a quote," yelled Jim Welch. "You'll have to give me ten strokes the next time we play golf!" shouted Tom Matte. "Hey, Willie," said Don Shula, "you're getting more attention than you did when you broke the color line at the North-South game." Shula's reference was to the fact that Willie had been one of two Negroes who had been the first of their race ever to play in that game. That followed his great years at Jackson State, and precipitated a parade for Willie in his home town of Greenville, Mississippi, another first for a Negro.

But following those good years came the bad years before Willie Richardson reached his maturity. He admits now that some of his pre-1965 troubles stemmed from the fact that he wasn't always in the best condition. He liked to party until he settled down and married in '65. Now he and his wife Sonji are the parents of a son and daughter, the owners of a nice house in a Baltimore suburb and two cars, and Willie is looking to the future. He has a twice-a-week radio program in Baltimore and would like to expand his work in that medium in the years ahead. But he also wants to firmly establish himself as a top receiver in the NFL now, because he knows one fine season didn't do it for him.

And now that John Unitas and the rest of the Colts have confidence in him, Willie should get to throw a few more footballs into the stands before he's finished.

DAVE ROBINSON Late last season *Sport Magazine* conducted a secret poll of the game scouts for every team in the National Football League and had them rate the top players, position by position. This was the report on Dave Robinson of the Green Bay Packers:

The best corner linebacker in the league, by far. Can really stay with the halfback or fullback coming out of the backfield for a pass, meets the tight end real well and can get away from sucker blocks. Has good speed shooting in on the passer, but is a little better against the pass than the run.

The one element the scouts left out in assessing what makes the 6'3", 240-pound Robinson such an outstanding football player is his aggressiveness, intelligently applied. Phil Bengtson, the new Packer head coach who for years was the team's defensive coach, says of Dave: "No one

I've met in pro football has within him a higher degree of intelligence and a higher capability of aggressiveness than Dave Robinson."

A Penn State graduate who works as a civil engineer in the off-season, Dave is a former tournament bridge player and a current chess buff. The way he plays both is indicative of the way he plays football. Listen to him discuss his style in chess:

"I don't like to checkmate," Dave says. "I'll see a checkmate and I'll let it go by. I'd rather destroy my opponent's knights and rooks. Destroy, destroy, destroy his weaponry until he's got nothing left."

Aggressiveness, intelligence, plus the ability to react instantly under pressure—these are the keys to Dave Robinson's skills on a football field. There was that play he made in the game against the Giants in New York last season which summed up all the skills of Dave Robinson. Giant quarterback Fran Tarkenton took the snap from center, spun and stuck the ball into the stomach of his halfback, Ernie Koy. Robinson moved toward the line to stop the run, which must have thrilled Tarkenton no end, because the play wasn't a run at all. He pulled the ball away from Koy on his nice fake and dashed back to pass, looking for his flankerback, Joe Morrison, who was running a turnout toward the sideline—the short area Dave Robinson was supposed to cover on a pass.

But Robinson, reacting instantly and utilizing the deceptive speed in his huge body, was now running toward the sideline, too, angling between the quarterback and his receiver. Just as Tarkenton released the ball, Robinson flashed into the passing plane and swung his big hand at the ball. It didn't hit it, but it did screen Morrison's vision for an instant, and the ball caromed off his thigh pad. Robinson, closing on Morrison, grabbed the rebound for the interception.

"I think linebacking is the most difficult job on the football field," Robinson told writer John Devaney last season. "A lineman worries about stopping runs. A deep back worries about stopping passes. A linebacker's got to worry about stopping runs *and* passes.

"When you say a quarterback is out to fool a defense, what you mean is that a quarterback is out to fool the linebackers. The quarterback knows what the front four will do: rush. And he doesn't have time to fool the deep backs. He's out to make three linebackers think *pass!* He gives the ball to a back and he has running room. Or he's out to make you think *run!* You rush up and the receivers go by you. So you got to read the play. You got to read the keys. And read them quick—no more than two seconds. You see a guard pull, a back come at you, you got to decide right then—pass or run? The keys are real and they are *right now.*"

Naturally, as a Packer, Robinson is fortunate in working with outstanding football players. He plays behind defensive end Willie Davis, one of the game"s all-time greats, and behind Dave himself, on the outside, is cornerback Herb Adderley and, on the inside, safetyman Tom Brown. Robinson and Davis team to string out the sweeps, push them out to the sideline until the deep backs and pursuit can get over to drop the ballcarrier. He helps the backs on passes by providing what the pros call "underneath coverage," that is, taking anything within ten to 15 yards from the line of scrimmage. This, of course, allows the backs to play a bit looser and thus minimizes the chances of a deep pass getting by them.

But in order to do his job Dave Robinson, linebacker, must never allow himself to be knocked off his feet. He must not let those tackles or backs or tight ends get into him with blocks. Which is why you will see him on any Sunday afternoon in the fall swinging his heavy forearms to smash down the people who would try to take away his legs. "Down there," Dave says, "It is a blood bath. Someone's always out to stick a linebacker."

This is fine with Dave Robinson, who plays it tough and expects opponents to play him tough. "The guys who hit me the hardest, I respect the most," Dave says. "John Mackey [the Colts' tight end] is one of my best friends. Our wives are very close. But I want to hit John hard so he will say after a game: 'Dave's his same old self. He played good ball out there today.' I wouldn't want to have as a friend a guy who played patsy with me out there."

"People say to me: 'Why do you try to hurt a man?' I don't try to hurt anyone out there. But I'll tell you this—if I have to run over a man's hand or take a chance on injuring myself by twisting out of his way, I'll run over that man's hand. And maybe in the fourth period he'll drop a pass because of that bad hand. The harder you hit a man in the first period, the more you slow him down in the fourth period. Also, the harder you hit someone, the less it hurts you."

During the 1966 season Robinson was thinking that if he got into the Super Bowl it would be worth as much as $16,000 to him and every one of his teammates. As it turned out, it was worth $25,000 to him and each of the other Packers. But he was figuring $16,000, which averaged out to $1000 per game, and that's how much he felt the opposition was trying to steal from him in each game. So he equated the opposition with common thieves and decided to treat them as such, like a thief he'd caught climbing out of his window with $1000 of his money.

"When someone on another team asks why I am so hard on them," Dave says, "I tell them about that thief. I say, 'What would you do if you caught that thief stuck in your window with your money?' They understand."

It is understandable why Dave Robinson made All-Pro linebacker the last two years, too. He consistently makes the big play. In December of 1965, the Packers met the Colts with the Western Conference title at stake. The Packers were leading 14-13, but the Colts had marched to Green Bay's two-yard line with 60 seconds on the clock till half-time. Gary Cuozzo, filling in for the injured John Unitas, called the play and Robinson expected a run. But when he saw tight end Mackey release from the line and the fullback swing out for a pass, he dashed for the sideline. Cuozzo tried to loop the pass over Robinson's head, but Dave can leap ten feet and did. He intercepted and ran the ball back 87 yards. The Packers, who seconds before had been in danger of trailing 20-14, scored to go ahead 21-13. "It was a 14-point play by Robinson and the turning point of the game," Vince Lombardi said afterward.

In 1966 Robinson made another turning-point play to beat the Colts and give the Packers the Conference title. With less than a minute to play the Packers led 14-10, but this time John Unitas was leading the Colts and he had them on the Green Bay 23 and moving. On first down Unitas faded to pass, found his receivers covered and raced up the middle. Robinson, out in the flat protecting against the pass, knew his job was to keep Unitas from getting to the sideline, "try to pin him inside where the big boys can stick him and maybe make him cough up the ball."

Dave did just that, and Willie Davis hit Unitas from an angle and made him fumble. Robinson, racing over, saw the ball pop loose, saw it hit the ground and bounce toward him. He dove on it, and the Packers had another conference title.

His biggest play of all, television fans will recall, was in the NFL championship game against Dallas. The Packers were leading by six points with less than a minute to play, but the Cowboys had the ball on Green Bay's two-yard line. Quarterback Don Meredith ran to his right on an option pass, looking for his flanker, Bob Hayes. Robinson held up Hayes at the line momentarily and Meredith stepped up as if to run. Dave crashed in, powering past guard Roger Donohue and hit Meredith just as his passing arm swept forward. The ball hung in the air and Tom Brown intercepted it. The Packers had another NFL title.

Robinson made similarly important plays all last season. Then, in the Pro Bowl, he earned the Outstanding Lineman Of The Game award for his overall performance in the Western Conference victory. Probably his biggest play came in the first half. The West was trailing 13-10 as the East took over the ball on their ten. East quarterback Fran Tarkenton scrambled out of the pocket and Willie Davis hit him so hard the ball popped loose. As usual, Dave Robinson was in perfect position to recover the bouncing ball.

Ironically, Robinson never felt he'd ever attain his present pre-eminence. He was a number one draft choice in 1963 after making All-America as a defensive end at Penn State, but he always had an uncertain attitude about his abilities to do much as a pro. "I never thought I'd last in the pros more than five years," Dave says. "And I never thought I'd stay with the Packers. But I figured I was lucky to be starting at the top. I thought I might sift down until I found my proper level, either in the NFL or with an AFL team."

He got to play a bit as a rookie due to injuries to veterans, but showed only raw ability. He played even more the next year, 1964, until a knee injury sidelined him, but again he showed he had a lot to learn. Even early in '65, when he became a regular after veteran Dan Currie was traded, Robinson still had trouble.

"I'd read pass on almost every play," he recalls. "I ran back any time the quarterback showed me pass action. There were always acres of grass in front of me.

"Now I feel things. I'll see one, two, three keys that say run, but I'll *feel* pass. Then I'll see the last key and know I was right: It's pass."

Then Dave Robinson will turn and run to his pass-coverage area and either knock down the pass or intercept it or hit the receiver so hard after the catch that he will drop the ball or think about Dave Robinson the next time he has to run a route in his vicinity. Which is exactly what you would expect "the best corner linebacker in the league, by far," to do.

GALE SAYERS If you judge by the rushing and pass-receiving statistics alone—and those are the general guidelines used to rate the top offensive halfbacks in pro football—Gale Sayers of the Chicago Bears had an "off" year in 1967. He rushed 186 times for 880 yards (which placed him third in the league) and seven touchdowns, and caught 16 passes for 126 yards and one touchdown. Remember, this is the fellow who as a rookie in '65 scored an all-time NFL record of 22 touchdowns, and who in '66 led the league in rushing with 1231 yards while gaining a record total of 2440 yards for the season in all offensive categories.

However, Gale Sayers did not have an "off" year in '67. In fact, he had a great year. The Bears had an off year, though. Consider their game against the Pittsburgh Steelers on September 17, 1967, for example. Sayers got the Bears six points almost before the game started. He ran back the opening kickoff 103 yards. He returned another kickoff 42 yards to give Chicago excellent field position.

He also carried the ball from scrimmage seven times ... and gained a grand total of *two* yards.

Yet after the football game, in the Steeler locker room, everyone was talking about Gale Sayers. "He really scares you," said defensive coach Vern Torgeson. "He's the best I've seen in a long time." "A fantastic football player," said head coach Bill Austin. "I don't think there's one better anywhere. I'm glad we came out alive."

But Austin also pointed to the game stat sheet and noted: "Look, here's why we won. We had 73 plays on offense to their 35."

And Bear coach George Halas said of his team: "Well, the facts are these, gentlemen. We made six major mistakes: two fumbles and one interception in the first half, two fumbles and one interception in the second half. When you run less than 40 plays ..."

There were other mistakes that Halas didn't mention, such as the flare pattern Sayers ran and got wide open on, with nothing ahead of him except the goal posts and then quarterback Rudy Bukich threw the ball over Gale's head. "Plays like that hurt us, too," Sayers admitted.

Plays like that hurt the Bears much of the season. In the 16-team National Football League, the Bears ranked 14th in passing. If you can't pass, defensive lines don't have to charge all-out on every play to try to get to the quarterback fast. They can sit back and play the run, and the linebackers can wait right behind the rush men, too. No matter how good a ball carrier is, it is very difficult for him to beat a tight four-three defense. As Pittsburgh proved against Sayers.

The previous week Gale had had a big game against the Cardinals, and the Steelers saw in the game films that the hard-charging St. Louis linemen had blown in so quickly that often Sayers blew by them before they could react. As Steeler defensive tackle Ken Kortas said, "The Cardinals have a charging team and they charged themselves right out of the game." Torgeson added: "We weren't as aggressive as we normally are. We tried not to give him any holes."

From the Steeler game on, defenses tried to follow the same pattern to stop Sayers and the Bears. And George Halas' team was not only passer poor, it fielded an inexperienced offensive line, a line that was being rebuilt and one that also suffered considerable injuries. This was another problem faced by Gale Sayers last season. He had to find his own holes, and entire defenses could be set up—and were—to stop him alone.

Nevertheless, Gale Sayers managed quite nicely most of the time, thank you. Ask the Detroit Lions, who have one of the better defensive teams in football. In their game against the Bears on October 15, they had to stop only four Chicago passes. That's four, count 'em. Halas said later it had to be the fewest that one of his teams had ever thrown in modern times. The field was so wet from the rain that poured down on Wrigley Field all afternoon that most players could get no traction whatsoever.

But Gale Sayers isn't like most players. Even though he limped so badly from the previous week's game when he reported to practice on Tuesday that he was excused from workouts all week, he was ready on Sunday. He rushed the ball 22 times and gained 142 yards.

"The doctor [Bear physician Ted Fox] told me all I could do was jog late in the week," said Gale. "And he told me only to jog straight ahead, not to try any cutting. I didn't know how well I could cut until the game. But I didn't have the knee bandaged because I didn't want to restrict my movements. I just made up my mind I wasn't going to think about my leg or the wet field."

His big run was a 70 yarder off left tackle. He followed fullback Ronnie Bull through the hole, made one of his famous hesitation moves to set up a block on the linebacker by his own wide end, Dick Gordon, and was gone.

Three weeks later the Lions had to face Sayers again. In this one he got off a 63-yard run from scrimmage despite an upset stomach that sent him to the bench afterward. "He was sick to his stomach," Lion defensive tackle Alex Karras said afterward. "He wasn't the only one. I threw up just watching it." Later Sayers returned a kickoff 97 yards for a touchdown, which made Karras' stomach even sicker but Gale's felt much better.

"We have a set pattern for our kickoffs," Sayers told reporters in the locker room. "We go up the middle, then break to the left or right, depending on how the other team is setting up. The movies showed us we might be able to go left on the Lions, and that's just what we did."

Teams had been kicking away from Sayers consistently, so he was told to line up in the end zone behind Dick Gordon, the team's other kick returner. When the ball was kicked, Sayers would run over and catch it, with Gordon leading the interference. Several teams took to not kicking long to Bears at all. Sayers told a Monday morning Giant quarterback club he thought this was a mistake because kicking short gave the Bears good field position.

Giant quarterback Fran Tarkenton agreed with the general rule that it's not a good idea to give opponents field position. "If you make a mistake inside the 20 you're in real trouble," said Fran. "Anything can kill you there. Naturally if you start on the 40 you can swing, you can open up the game and go. But you have to remember—there's still 60 yards to go." Which, Tarkenton decided, was better than kicking to Sayers and chancing a touchdown in a matter of seconds, as happened to Pittsburgh and Detroit.

"I don't know," said the unconvinced Sayers. "Green Bay kicked short to us. We got the ball on the 40 once and went to a touchdown. We lost 13-10, but it was pretty close.

"The Rams didn't kick to me, either. They were short and we scored off one of them."

"Who won the game?" asked Fran.

"L.A. did, 28-17," Gale said.

"The prosecution rests," said Tarkenton.

You would think the 49ers would have agreed with the prosecution. They had had all kinds of trouble stopping Sayers going into their December 3, 1967, game with the Bears. He had scored six touchdowns in one rookie game against them and had gained 697 yards in 66 attempts in the games against the 49ers that followed. But they didn't learn. They kicked off to Sayers to open that December '67 game and Gale promptly ran back the high floater 97 yards to a touchdown. That gave him six touchdowns on kickoff returns in three seasons, to tie Ollie Matson's all-time NFL career TD record. Matson set his in 14 seasons.

Sayers returned two other kickoffs for 48 yards against the 49ers and ran back a punt 58 yards for a touchdown. Although San Francisco did do a good job of holding down Sayers from scrimmage, limiting him to 30 yards in

11 carries, he also scored a touchdown through the line. Once again he had a big day on a muddy field that had most of the players slipping and sliding when they cut. Why not Sayers? What makes him so great on a wet playing surface?

"I cut on my heels," says Sayers, "and that helps me keep my footing in the mud. Most backs cut on the balls of their feet. Actually, I hate a muddy field. There are a lot of things you can't do, like trying to sweep the ends. You can only run off tackle and use traps."

Sayers' touchdown run from scrimmage started as a play off right tackle, except a blitzing linebacker ran into the hole as he reached the line. Somehow Gale stopped short in the mud and turned the play into a run around the left end for the 15-yard score. It was a fantastic bit of body control, cutting ability, speed and instinct, which pretty much sums up the skills of Gale Sayers.

Small wonder that in a secret poll of NFL scouts conducted by *Sport Magazine* to determine the top players, by position, in the NFL, Gale Sayers was the lone unanimous pick of the scouts. Said one of them: "He's in the Hall of Fame already. If he stopped playing tomorrow, his place would be secure." People like Gale Sayers don't have "off" years even if their teams are not quite what they might be.

BART STARR During the 1966 National Football League season, quarterback Bart Starr of the Green Bay Packers gave up exactly three interceptions. That's three. It was a fantastic record even for Starr, who has always been among the league leaders in fewest interceptions allowed.

However, in the first two games of the 1967 season, Bart Starr gave up nine interceptions. Many people seized upon this fact to proclaim that Starr had lost it as a passer, that he was 34 years old now and that it had happened to other quarterbacks when they reached that age. The arm becomes a little weaker, the reflexes a bit slower, and in the precision game that is professional football today, little things mean a lot.

But knowledgeable football people felt Starr's skills couldn't have faded so fast. More likely, the belief was, Starr was hurt. Not hurt bad enough for Vince Lombardi to sit him on the bench in favor of 36-year-old Zeke Bratkowski at quarterback, but hurt just enough to hamper his performance.

Events soon proved the latter suspicion correct. In game number three, Starr was his old self, hitting passes all over the field, calling the perfect play almost every time, faking nicely, and the whole team was picked up as the Packers easily beat Atlanta. But in the next few games Starr again looked bad.

Finally Lombardi announced that Starr would not play the following week, that he was hurt and had been all season that he had been unfair in playing Bart so long but that he'd felt he had to. Ever since the second game of the season, it turned out, Starr had been suffering with painfully damaged ribs, a pulled thigh muscle and an injured right hand that affected his grip on the football. The rib injury limited the freedom of his passing arm and the pulled thigh muscle hampered his setting up to throw. Small wonder Starr was playing badly.

When you consider the fact that the Packers' running game was also in trouble, the most amazing thing was that the Packers weren't losing more games. Never in the history of the Packers under Vince Lombardi had the team depended so much on one ballplayer, Bart Starr, and he was only periodically effective.

Jerry Kramer, the veteran Packer All-League guard, was talking in the pre-season about the evolution of the Packers and just how much Starr meant to the team now. "In recent years the burden has fallen more and more on Bart," said Jerry. "Always before it was Jimmy Taylor and Paul Hornung [the great fullback and halfback who had made Green Bay such a formidable running team in other years, but who were Packers no longer in 1967]. And our offensive line was big and strong and it could overpower almost anybody. Now Jimmy and Paul are gone and the burden is on Bart Starr. It's all on Bart

Starr. He carries the whole thing and we're not as strong and as quick as we used to be on the offensive line."

Which is one reason why opposing rush lines were putting more pressure than ever on Starr, tipping his passes or smashing him to the ground just as he released the ball. This not only contributed to Starr's inordinately high interception total; more importantly it contributed to his inordinate number of injuries. Even before the season opened, following the exhibition games, Starr himself said, "I've never started training in better shape . . . and I've never had so many annoying little injuries."

As noted, though, despite the injuries Starr kept playing as long as he could. He felt the burden, this man who has always been so quiet and so nice, and he asserted himself. Most people have no idea of the changes Bart Starr has had to go through in recent years as leadership of the Packers has been thrust more and more on his shoulders. It is a measure of his adaptability and ability the way he has responded to the burdens. First of all you must realize that Bart Starr has never thought of himself as a Johnny Unitas, a guy who virtually all by himself could carry a football team. Starr realizes quite realistically that he just doesn't have the physical equipment of a Unitas, the very strong arm, the very quick release, the deadly accuracy over a full season, the extremely strong leadership skills. But beginning a few years ago the leader in Starr began to come out.

"Five years ago I wouldn't go up to a rookie to urge him to do the best job he could on the special teams," Starr told writer Leonard Shecter last season. "Or I wouldn't say something to some guy who may not even be in the game. Like: 'Look, if you get a call, be sure you're darn ready, be prepared.' I wouldn't find myself saying these things because at the time there were other people to be saying these things to him. You [Bart often modestly refers to himself as "you" or "we"] were *not* a senior ranking member of the squad. But as time goes on and you become a senior member of the team, you realize that it's your responsibility to say these things or they won't get said. You know, the coaches can say only so much to a player. After that it's the responsibility of the guys on the club."

It wasn't an easy thing for Starr to assert his leadership,

because it just isn't his nature to be a hard leader. But this is not to imply that he isn't by nature a stand-up guy.

"There is a softness in him," Jerry Kramer says, "a sort of gentle manliness. But there is also an iron-hard spirit. I recall when we were playing the Bears about five years ago. Bill George [the big, tough Chicago middle linebacker then] came through and hit Bart in the mouth. A real good shot. Blood all over. 'That'll take care of you, kid,' George said. You should have seen Bart. He snarled right back. Challenged him right there. 'You big bum,' Bart says, and he's ready to fight. That's one thing about this game: you have to be ready to fight, and Bart always is."

But Starr was not as aggressive with teammates in those days, even when he probably should have been. "A few years ago," Kramer continues, "if he felt he had to say something to one of us, something like, 'C'mon, Jerry, let's go," he'd come up after the game and say, 'Sorry, I didn't mean to holler at you.' Now he'll say, 'Darn it, you should have caught that ball,' or 'Heck, if I'd had a little more time I could've hit somebody with that pass.' He has the iron in him and he's more willing to express it now."

Express it he does, particularly at the most crucial times, just as he plays at the crucial times, hurt or not. He was injured, as noted, most of last season, and had not played up to his usual standards as a result. But by the time the Western Conference title game was played, Starr was ready. Lombardi rested him in the season's finale against the Pittsburgh Steelers (the Packers lost), saving him for the winner of the Ram-Colt game. The powerful Rams won and many experts felt they had the momentum to beat Green Bay a week later. Starr led the Packers to an easy victory.

The NFL championship against the Cowboys was something else again, played in 13-below-zero temperatures in Green Bay. After Starr passed for two touchdowns in the first 18 minutes, hitting flanker Boyd Dowler from eight and 46 yards out, the Cowboys took over. They scored ten points in the second quarter and seven more in the fourth period.

Meanwhile, Dallas' front four were dropping Starr all over the football field. They tackled him eight times for losses totaling 76 yards. Once Starr fumbled and the loose ball was run into the end zone by Cowboy defensive end George Andrie. The Cowboy rush line was playing with so much fire that few people really expected Starr to mount much of an attack when he regained the ball with five minutes to play.

But attack Starr did, throwing mostly to his backs coming out of the backfield, because the frozen field provided no running traction. This limited Starr's ground game, but it also limited the ability of the Dallas linebackers to cover his flaring backs. Calling his plays carefully and passing expertly, Starr marched the team 65 yards to the Dallas three. Then he called on halfback Donny Anderson for two crashes into the line. But the Cowboys rose up and stopped him at the one.

There were 16 seconds on the clock and Starr had no time-outs left, but he didn't hesitate. He called a quarterback sneak in the huddle and told his teammates, "We darn well better make it, too."

He made it, driving into the end zone between blocks thrown by Jerry Kramer and center Bob Hyland. "I knew it was probably our last play," Bart said later. "But the traction wasn't good—Donny Anderson had slipped on the previous play—and I knew the backs might have trouble getting started. That's why I decided to keep the ball."

He won the game, as he won the Super Bowl two weeks later over the AFL champion Oakland Raiders. In this one, Bart won his second successive Corvette, awarded annually by *Sport Magazine* to the most valuable player in the world championship game. It was a fitting finish for a guy who had to show a few people that he hadn't slipped as a football player.

CHARLEY TAYLOR

When he was a member of the great Arizona State backfield that featured him at halfback and Tony Lorick, now of the Colts, at fullback, Charley Taylor had one goal in life. It was a very large goal indeed, but what was the point in setting goals at all if they weren't large ones, Charley figured. Taylor's goal was to become as outstanding a running back in the National Football League as Jimmy Brown was, and, of course, Jimmy brown was the best the game had ever seen.

But his goal was not beyond Charley Taylor, because he had a lot going for him. He had size at 6′3″, 215 pounds, speed (9.9 in the 100), shiftiness afoot, power, determination—all the credentials to become a great running back. And he started like one. Drafted number one by the Washington Redskins in 1964, Charley went on to become the National Football League's Rookie-of-the-Year. Playing offensive halfback, he rushed for 755 yards (the sixth highest total in the league) and caught 53 passes (ranking eighth) for 814 yards. No other rookie had finished among the top ten in rushing and receiving in 21 years. Experts predicted a great future for Charley Taylor, halfback.

But in 1965 Taylor injured an ankle in the pre-season and the injury lingered through the season, which was not a good one for Charley. He didn't look like the same ballplayer. His average gain per carry dropped from 3.8 yards to 2.8.

The following year, Charley felt, would be different. His ankle was healed and the young Redskin line which had had many problems in '65 just had to be better. Taylor figured on not only returning to his rookie form but surpassing it.

But early in 1966 Charley Taylor, halfback, didn't look a whole lot better than he had in '65. And Otto Graham, who had taken over as the Redskin coach that season, wasn't about to waste a great athlete like Taylor at halfback if he couldn't do the job, because Graham was convinced Charley Taylor could become one of the finest wide receivers in the league. Despite his troubles as a runner—20 yards in 11 carries, nine yards in six carries, three yards in seven carries in successive games—Charley was still catching a lot of passes, particularly short ones which he turned into long gains. So Graham began alternating Taylor at halfback and at split end. Then, in the ninth game of the '66 season, he made Taylor a fulltime split end; Charley would not carry the ball from scrimmage anymore. Charley was stunned.

It was a trying time for Taylor and a ticklish situation for the Redskins, if you recall the background of the Graham-Taylor relationship. Graham coached Taylor before, on the College All-Star squad in '64, and one day Otto told a writer: "Charley is a great athlete, but he is very lazy. He comes late for practice and he is the first to leave. He even misses practice ... he seems to have no interest."

Taylor never forgot those words. In fact, when he won the Rookie-of-the-Year award that season he said to a writer: "Is Otto Graham still in football?"

Now Graham was again his coach, and the man who was taking away his chance of ever fulfilling his goal. "To lose it all of a sudden," Taylor told writer John Devaney for a *Sport Magazine* story last season, "after you've set out to do something and come so close ... it's got to take something out of you. I'd come home from practice and I'd be so upset and worried I couldn't eat. My weight fell to 195. There was a big ball of worry in my mind."

"I didn't expect him to be overjoyed with the switch," Graham says. "Charley is a great athlete, but the more I looked at him, the more I was convinced he would never be a great running back. Charley doesn't have the temperament for the position; he's too impatient. He wouldn't wait for the pattern of a play to develop. He'd run ahead of the interference on traps, for instance, and the man who was supposed to be trapped would be there waiting for him. Charley never learned to glide, to run under control. He couldn't force himself to do it. We noticed that his best runs were to the outside, where he just outran people."

Some people felt that Taylor's troubles running inside were the result of lack of courage, that subconsciously at least he wasn't sticking his head in the hole with his original, pre-injury verve. These hints plagued Taylor, who felt that all he needed was a little patience from the coaches to regain his form.

"The coaches would show me films," Charley says, 'and they'd say, 'Look, you're dancing in that hole; you got to boom your way through.' I knew what the coaches were thinking—that I was afraid to hit that hole, that I was worried about that ankle. I knew I was doing a lot of dancing. I hadn't got over those injuries to my ankle at that time. The older you get and the longer you play, the longer it takes to get over something like that. Like in college when I had a broken neck. I had to get over it. I kept saying to myself: I got over worrying about my neck and I'll get over worrying about my ankle. But it would take time. The coaches wouldn't give me that time."

Taylor, once he'd been switched to split end in game number nine of '66, was also worried about the complexities of the new position. He was an instinctive running back, and he didn't have to worry about making a mistake there. But split end was a whole new area to him, a job that required running precise patterns, reading defenses, beating double coverage, reacting instantly to shifting coverages.

Redskin flanker Bobby Mitchell, who had made the position shift himself some years before, tried to help Taylor. Says Bobby: "It's not hard for a good running back to be a good receiver. Heck, Charley was darn near leading the team in receiving as a halfback when he made the switch. But there are differences. A halfback is used to having the ball going away from him when he comes out of the backfield for a pass. A receiver, he's running *toward* the ball a lot of times, or the ball is coming to him at an angle.

"Another thing: a halfback usually is covered by a linebacker, who'll run to a certain spot and sit there. It's a set thing; you know what the linebacker will do. But when you're a receiver being covered by a defensive back, you have to make him react—and react wrong—to one of your moves. In other words, you got to run a lot more complicated patterns."

And, of course, the comedown felt by a running back who's asked to shift to receiver can be very bad. Mitchell himself didn't like the idea when it was first proposed to him, and Timmy Brown hated it when the Eagles experimented with him at flanker.

"A running back, you love that position," says Mitchell. "If you have the size, the speed, the elusiveness, that is the premier position. A halfback can run with the ball, he can catch the ball, he can pass the ball. And at halfback you *know* you will be in the game. The quarterback has to hand off to you. A receiver, all he can do is catch the ball. And he might be double-teamed and the quarterback may never throw the ball to him for an entire game. Before a game a halfback can say to himself: 'I *know* I'm going to have a good game.' All a receiver can say is: 'I *hope* I'm going to have a good game.' "

So Charley Taylor made the switch and had a good game. He caught eight passes for 111 yards and a touchdown. Then, against the Cowboys, he had another good game, catching 11 passes to tie Mitchell's one-game team record. Then he had another good game, and another, and another. . . .

By the end of the season Charley Taylor had caught 72 passes—more than anyone else in the NFL. Fifty-four of them had come in the last six games of the year—a truly incredible statistic.

But when he reported to training camp in 1967 Charley Taylor had to forget that he had led the league in receiving six months earlier. "If I had come to camp carrying that on my shoulders—best pass-catcher in the league—I would have come in with my head all swollen and I wouldn't have learned anything," Taylor told a writer midway through the season. "I came to camp willing to learn the fundamentals of the position."

There had been some criticism of Taylor the halfback for kidding around too much in practice. But that, the kidding around and the criticism, ended once he became a split end. "He definitely has a different attitude about football now," Graham says. "He is a much more serious football player."

Taylor himself admits this is true, that he was gifted with the skills of a running back and didn't have to concentrate so hard in workouts. "Being an end," he says, "was something I had to learn myself. I was starting from the ground up. I knew I had to do extra work. I couldn't afford not to. I know I clown around less. I'll only fool around now when I have everything down perfect."

In '66 he ran simple patterns, mostly square-outs and little turn-ins over the middle. (Television viewers will never forget one such pass he caught against the Cowboys. Three of them hit him, had him cold, except that Taylor broke the tackles and dropped the football in the end zone 78 yards away.) In '67 he knew that defenses would set up to stop him, that they would take away his turn-outs and turn-ins unless he tacked some new moves on the end of them. Redskin end coach Ray Renfro worked hard all through training camp and through the exhibition season helping Taylor perfect new moves, new patterns, and quarterback Sonny Jurgensen stayed late to get the routes timed up precisely.

Once the season opened it was apparent that Charley Taylor was a much better split end than he had been the previous season. He still was not a real good pattern runner, because he was still primarily an instinctive football player. His great running was done *after* he caught the ball, whereas most receivers are just the opposite—they run to get open, shake the defender, but they are not particularly good runners with the football in the open field.

Charley Taylor is a great runner in the open field, when danger is all about him, threatening to smash him into the earth. One play against the Eagles illustrated this. A linebacker was set up to chuck him at the line, hold him up, but Charley broke free, sliced across the middle and took Jurgensen's seven-yard pass. He was hit by two Eagles. Charley spun loose. Five steps and another defender tackled him around the waist. Charley shrugged him off. Ten more yards and three more Eagles converged on him. Twisting and straining, Charley again wriggled free. Seven yards farther and two more Eagles hit him. Charley shed one and dragged the other a full five yards before three more defenders leaped on his back.

Altogether, Charley Taylor had been hit by 11 Eagles, but had still managed to carry a seven-yard pass 39 yards. What will he do when he becomes a better pattern runner?

You see, in 1967 Charley Taylor again led the National Football League in receiving, catching 70 passes for 990 yards and nine touchdowns. But, deep down, he'd probably still rather be a running back.

JOHNNY UNITAS The 1967 National Football League season was probably the most disappointing Johnny Unitas has ever gone through. The Colt quarterback, almost all by himself, led his team to an undefeated record through the first 13 games of the schedule—the longest undefeated streak in the NFL since 1934. Going into the final game of the season, the Colts had won 11 games and tied two. However, the Colts next opponent, the Los Angeles Rams, had won ten games, tied two and lost one. So the entire season's play in the newly aligned Coastal Division came down to this one final game. Because the divisional winner was to be decided, in the event that two teams finished with identical records, by the total number of points the tied teams scored against one another. The Colts and Rams had played to a 28-28 tie in their first meeting, which meant if the Rams could beat the Colts in their last game, they would earn the right to play the Green Bay Packers, winners of the Central Division title (with a 9-4-1 record), for the Western Conference championship.

In essence, the game pitted Unitas—who had already been voted the Most-Valuable-Player in the NFL—against the most terrifying front four in the league. It was led by David (Deacon) Jones, a 6'5", 260-pound All-Pro defensive end who had finished second to Unitas in the MVP voting, and 6'5", 275-pound All-Pro defensive tackle Merlin Olsen. And it was filled out by 6'5", 290-pounder former three-time All-Pro defensive tackle Roger Brown and 6'7", 260-pound Lamar Lundy, thought by many to be the most underrated defensive end in the league. This group can put more pressure on a quarterback than any in football. And they knew they would have to stop Unitas.

"He is the greatest quarterback I ever played against," Jones said two days before the game. "Some quarterbacks, if you hit them hard a couple of times early, they begin to hear the footsteps—they begin to look for you instead of the receivers. So we'll get to Unitas as much as we can. But we know he doesn't care about the footsteps, which is what makes him great. He keeps his eyes on the receivers even when he knows you're about to break him in half."

Said Olsen: "Once in a while the defense gets there, knocks down Unitas, stomps on him, hurts him. The test of a quarterback is what he does next. Unitas gets up, calls another pass and drops back into the pocket. Out of the corner of his eye he may see you coming. And I swear that when he does he holds that ball a split second longer than he really has to—just to let you know he isn't afraid of any man. Then he throws it on the button. . . . No position in any sport requires more ability or more courrage. I weigh 275, and I don't know if I could absorb the punishment that quarterbacks take."

Unitas absorbed a great deal of punishment in this game. The Colt line had been rebuilt with youngsters before the season, and even during the season when Jim Parker had to quit. But they had done an amazing job of protecting Unitas, allowing opponents to drop him for losses only 18 times in the first 13 games. However, the Ram front four was not to be held out on this day. They tackled Unitas with the ball seven times, and put so much pressure on him the rest of the time that he hardly had time to set up to throw. The Rams won 34-10. "They were murder," Johnny said in the locker room afterward. Then he smiled and added, "I'll try not to think about those four blanks all summer, but I guess I will."

As a professional, Unitas had to admire the work of the front four that beat him. But he did not have to admire the system which eliminated his Colts from contention after they had lost only once in 14 football games.

A few weeks later John said, "The new divisional setup was ridiculous. It's something that should be changed by the front office. But even with the divisional setup there should have been a playoff between the Colts and Rams for the Coastal title after we both finished with the same record. Sure the Rams chewed us up in that second game by putting a big rush on me. But could they have done it again a week later? I doubt it. The young fellows on the

Colts deserved a shot at the big money after we'd gone undefeated in 13 straight games."

Small wonder he was disappointed. Nevertheless, Unitas was very pleased with the way he'd come back from injuries the previous season, regaining the old form which a damaged shoulder had robbed him of during the second half of '66. John had the Colts tied for first place with the Packers then, each having 7-2 records. The next week he took his team to another win, beating the Atlanta Falcons, but he was smashed hard on one play in this game and hurt his throwing shoulder. The Colts won only two of the last six games of the season.

"The shoulder was the main reason for our offensive problems the last part of '66," John said early in '67. "I just couldn't put the speed on the ball that I wanted to, therefore allowing defensive men that fraction of a second needed to get to it."

This was why Unitas, who gave up just 12 interceptions in 1965, gave up 24 of them in '66. The shoulder responded to treatment and rest over the winter and was fine last season. He still had a lot of pain in his right elbow, though. It has been bothering him for several years.

"It's a problem of the tendon pulling away from the bone. Every time I throw the ball, it does it. But it doesn't bother me that much after I get warmed up and loose before a game. I don't throw as much in practice any more, though. Now I only work enough to stay sharp, maybe two or three days a week. There's a lot of pain, more now than last season. But I can live with the pain. The doctors aren't sure what an operation would do, and I'd rather live with the pain than take a chance on ruining the arm."

The Colt quarterback discovered when he viewed films of the second half of '66 games that he had unconsciously altered his throwing style, no doubt in deference to his injured shoulder. Historically, veteran quarterbacks have come down from an overhand style to a three-quarters or sidearm motion as they've grown older. It happens with baseball pitchers, too. The overhand motion apparently weakens the shoulder after a certain number of years.

"I didn't realize there had been a change," John said last season. "I have been concentrating on coming over the top more when I throw, and I'm also trying to concentrate on a good follow-through to get more zip on the ball with better control."

Whatever he did, it worked very well. Johnny Unitas threw more passes than anyone else in football except for Sonny Jurgensen of the Redskins who was forced to throw on virtually every play. And Unitas completed 255 of his 436 passes for the highest percentage in the league (and his best ever): 58.5. They were good for 3428 yards and 20 touchdowns. He allowed only 16 interceptions.

In the midst of perhaps his finest all-round performance ever, Unitas reached an all-time NFL career mark of over 30,000 yards gained passing. When a reporter told him he had passed for more than 17 miles as a pro, Johnny said, "Is that so? I guess I'm due for a 17-mile checkup and an oil change."

Typical of his play last season was Unitas' performance against the Packers, whom the Colts had not beaten in five successive games. It was a record they looked like they would extend when late in the game Green Bay led 10-0 and seemed in complete control. But Unitas finally got a march going. He passed to flanker Willie Richardson. He passed to split end Alex Hawkins. He passed to fullback Tony Lorick. There were two minutes and 19 seconds left to play when he hit Hawkins in the end zone. The point-after-touchdown kick was blocked, but the succeeding kickoff was not. Lou Michaels nubbed an on-side kick and Rich Volk, the ball-holder who had fouled up the PAT attempt, recovered for the Colts. They couldn't settle for a field goal; they had to get into the end zone or lose.

Now, with a minute and 56 seconds left to play, Unitas came up to the line of scrimmage, Green Bay's 34. Mixing his plays carefully, John got a first down on the 23 in four plays. Then he hit Richardson with the winning touchdown pass.

"How can you ever give up when you have Unitas going for you?" Hawkins said afterward. As long as we have that guy, I'll never believe we're out of any game until it's over."

As Packer coach Vince Lombardi says: "Unitas scares me every time he steps on a football field."

Which is why Unitas signed a three-year contract with the Colts last season that was reportedly worth $125,000 per season. That had to muffle his disappointment at not getting a piece of that big money in the championship games, but it didn't eliminate it because John was thinking of his young teammates when he criticized the new divisional setup. Of course, his concern for his teammates is just another reason for his greatness.

PHIL BENGTSON, Green Bay Packers

Blitzing teams like to send their weakside and middle line-backers in tandem—and quarterback Bart Starr loves to see this play coming. He reads and reacts to this blitz as well as any quarterback in the game. Starr calls for his fullback to pick up the middle backer and for his halfback to double up with his center on the dogging weakside line-backer. Under this ample protection he fires a quick pass over the middle to his split end, who is one-on-one with the cornerback and can turn this into a big play if the weak-side safety isn't back helping out in center field.

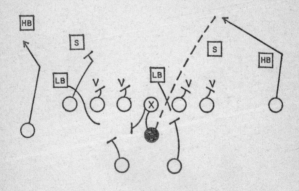

BLANTON, COLLIER, Cleveland Browns

Leroy Kelly is just as effective on this play as Jim Brown was—the strongside sweep. The strongside guard and running back Ernie Green, a fine blocker, leads the interference. Each hits the first opposing "color" he sees, though ideally the back takes the safety and the guard takes the cornerback. Another key block is thrown by the Browns' tight end on the strongside linebacker. Kelly takes the handoff from quarterback Frank Ryan and runs to daylight.

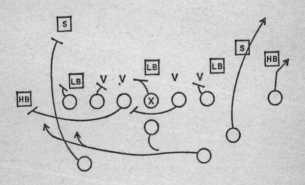

WEEB EWBANK, New York Jets

This is a standard—and very effective—pass call when the Jets anticipate a blitz. Quarterback Joe Namath keeps both of his backs in to block. Flanker Don Maynard is the primary receiver. He slants in, turns up, then to the sideline. He must make his moves and get open in no more than 2.5 seconds. If he's covered, Namath looks next to tight end Pete Lammons, who blocks down, then hooks over the middle. Split end George Sauer is the number three receiver on the weakside.

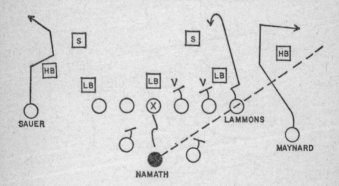

OTTO GRAHAM, Washington Redskins

This is one of the short passes that league-leading receiver Charley Taylor usually turns into long-gainers. From his split end position Taylor runs a quick turn-out to the sideline. Quarterback Sonny Jurgensen takes the snap and immediately fires to the flat before the cornerback can get up to stop the pass. The cornerback has to give Taylor the short throw or chance Charley's going deep on him. Once he has room, Taylor is one-on-one with the cornerback and can almost always get by any one man with his great moves.

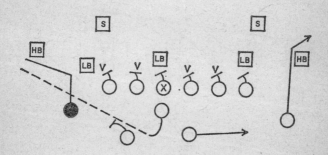

GEORGE HALAS, Chicago Bears

This is the play opponents know they must stop if they are
to stop the Bears—Gale Sayers on the quick pitch. The
Bears' strongside guard and tackle pull and combine with
the tight end's block on the linebacker to open the lane.
The Chicago quarterback takes the snap, whirls and tosses
the ball to Sayers—who tends to make the play go even
when all the blocks are not crisp. He has even reversed his
field when the defense has gotten over too quickly, dashing
around the then open weak side.

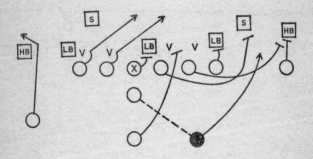

MIKE HOLOVAK, Boston Patriots

This is one of the up-the-middle plays that has helped Jim Nance lead the American Football League in rushing for two successive years. The blocking is optional; that is, the linemen drive their opponents whichever way the rush men initially go. Nance takes the handoff and picks his route through the line as the hole develops, then cuts to daylight in the secondary.

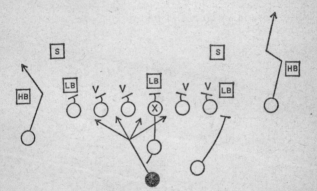

ALLIE SHERMAN, New York Giants

Undoubtedly the most spectacular play of last season was devised by creative Giant coach Al Sherman. It beat the Steelers and caused Pittsburgh coach Bill Austin to call what the Giants refer to as the Wellington (Mara) Special "a high-school play." Quarterback Fran Tarkenton hands the ball to fullback Ernie Koy, who runs toward the strongside behind his halfback on what looks like a sweep. But flanker Homer Jones runs toward the weakside and takes the ball from Koy on what looks like a reverse. Only Jones flips the ball back to Tarkenton, who passes to split end Joe Morrison—who has filtered through the secondary all alone.

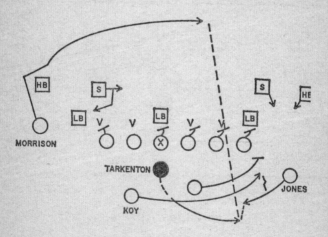

THE 1967 STATISTICS

THE CHAMPIONSHIPS

THE SUPER BOWL
January 16, 1968, at Miami

Green Bay	3	13	10	7—33
Oakland	0	7	0	7—14

GB—FG Chandler 39
GB—FG Chandler 20
GB—Dowler 63 pass from Starr (Chandler kick)
Oak—Miller 23 pass from Lamonica (Blanda kick)
GB—FG Chandler 43
GB—Anderson 2 run (Chandler kick)
GB—FG Chandler 31
GB—Adderley 60 pass interception (Chandler kick)
Oak—Miller 23 pass from Lamonica (Blanda kick)
Attendance—75,546

	Raiders	Packers
First downs	16	19
Rushing Yardage	105	163
Passing Yardage	186	162
Return Yardage	139	144
Passes	34-15-0	24-13-1
Punts	3-44	3-39
Fumbles Lost	2	0
Yards Penalized	31	12

INDIVIDUAL STATISTICS

Rushing Oakland—Dixon 12 carries for 52 yards, Todd 2-37, Banaszak 6-16. Total: 20-105 for 5.2 average no touchdowns.

Rushing, Green Bay—Wilson 17-65, Anderson 14-48 and 1 TD. Williams 8-36, Starr 1-14, Mercein 1-0. Totals: 41-163 for 4.0 average and 1 TD.

Passing, Oakland—Lamonica 15 of 34 for 208 yards, 2 TD and 1 interception.

Passing, Green Bay—Starr 13 of 24 for 202 yards, 1 TD and 0 interceptions. Bratkowski 0 for 0 for 0.

Lamonica and Starr thrown three times each attempting to pass. Bratkowski thrown once.

Pass receiving, Oakland—Miller 5 for 84 yards and 2 TD; Banaszak 4-69; Cannon 2-25; Wells 1-17; Dixon 1-3.

Pass receiving Green Bay—Dowler 2-17 and 1 TD; Dale 4-43; Fleming 4-35; McGee 1-35; Anderson 2-18.

1967 CHAMPIONSHIP PLAYOFFS
NATIONAL LEAGUE
December 31 at Green Bay, Wisconsin
GREEN BAY PACKERS (21)

Offensive Ends—Dowler, Dale, Fleming, Long, McGee.
Defensive Ends—Davis, Aldridge, B. Brown.
Offensive Tackles—Skoronski, Gregg, Wright.
Defensive Tackles—Kostelnik, Jordan, Weatherwax.
Guards—Kramer, Gillingham, Thurston.
Centers—Hyland, Bowman.

Linebackers—Nitschke, Robinson, Caffey, Crutcher, Flanigan.
Quarterbacks—Starr, Bratkowski, Horn.
Offensive Backs—Anderson, Mercein, Williams, Wilson.
Defensive Backs—Adderley, Jeter, T. Brown, Wood, Rowser, Hart.
Kicker—Chandler.

DALLAS COWBOYS (17)
Offensive Ends—Hayes, Rentzel, Stokes, Clarke.
Defensive Ends—Townes, Andrie, Stephens.
Offensive Tackles—Neely, Boeke.
Defensive Tackles—Lilly, Pugh, East.
Guards—Niland, Donohue, Liscio, Wilbur.
Centers—Connelly, Walker.
Linebackers—Jordan, Howley, Edwards, Hays, Tubbs.
Quarterbacks—Meredith, Morton, Rhome.
Offensive Backs—Reeves, Perkins, Baynham, Shy, Garrison.
Defensive Backs—Green, Johnson, Gaechter, Renfro, Clark, Daniels.
Kicker—Villanueva.

SCORING SUMMARY

Green Bay Packers	7	7	0	7—21
Dallas Cowboys	0	10	0	7—17

G.B.—Dowler, 8, pass from Starr (Chandler, kick).
G.B.—Dowler, 46, pass from Starr (Chandler, kick).
Dal.—Andrie, 7, fumble recovery (Villanueva, kick).
Dal.—FG, Villanueva, 21.
Dal.—Rentzel, 50, pass from Reeves (Villanueva, kick).
G.B.—Starr, 1, run (Chandler, kick).
Attendance—50,861.

INDIVIDUAL STATISTICS
Rushes—G.B.: Anderson, 18 for 35 yards; Mercein, 6 for 20; Williams, 4 for 13; Wilson, 3 for 11. Dal.: Perkins, 17 for 51; Reeves, 13 for 42.
Passes—G.B.: Starr, 14 of 24 for 191 yards. Dal.: Meredith, 10 of 25 for 59; Reeves, 1 of 1 for 50.
Receptions—G.B.: Dowler, 4 for 77 yards; Anderson, 4 for 44; Dale, 3 for 44; Mercein, 2 for 22. Dal.: Hayes, 3 for 16; Reeves, 3 for 11; Rentzel, 2 for 61; Clarke, 2 for 24.

TEAM STATISTICS

	Packers	Cowboys
First downs	18	11
Rushing yardage	80	92
Passing yardage	115	100
Return yardage	44	43
Passes	14-24	11-26
Interceptions by	1	0
Punts	8-29	8-39
Fumbles lost	2	1
Yards penalized	10	58

AMERICAN LEAGUE
December 31 at Oakland, California
OAKLAND RAIDERS (40)
Offensive Ends—Miller, Biletnikoff, Cannon, Wells, Sherman, Kocourek, Herock.
Defensive Ends—Davidson, Lassiter, Oats.
Offensive Tackles—Schuh, Svihus, Archer.
Defensive Tackles—Keating, Birdwell.
Guards—Hawkins, Upshaw, Harvey.
Centers—J. Otto, Kruse.
Linebackers—Conners, Laskey, G. Otto, Budness, Williamson, Benson.
Quarterbacks—Lamonica, Blanda.
Offensive Backs—Banaszak, Dixon, Todd, Hagberg.
Defensive Backs—McCloughan, Brown, Powers, Grayson, Williams, Bird.
Kicker—Eischeid.

HOUSTON OILERS (7)
Offensive Ends—Taylor, Burrell, Reed, Frazier, Bass, Poole.
Defensive Ends—Holmes, Marshall, Floyd.
Offensive Tackles—Suggs, Hines, Stith.
Defensive Tackles—Parker, G. Rice, A. Rice.
Guards—Talamini, Bishop, Regner.
Centers—Maples, Wittenborn.
Linebackers—Boyette, Webster, Underwood, Caveness, Barnes, Brabham.

Quarterbacks—Beathard, Davis, Anderson.
Offensive Backs—Campbell, Granger, Blanks, Hopkins.
Defensive Backs—Farr, Hicks, Houston, Norton, Moore, Jancik, Johns.

SCORING SUMMARY

Oakland Raiders	3	14	10	13—40
Houston Oilers	0	0	0	7— 7

Oak.—FG, Blanda, 37.
Oak.—Dixon, 69, run (Blanda, kick).
Oak.—Kocourek, 18, pass from Lamonica (Blanda, kick).
Oak.—Lamonica, 1, run (Blanda, kick).
Oak.—FG, Blanda, 40.
Oak.—FG, Blanda, 42.
Hou.—Frazier, 5, pass from Beathard (Wittenborn, kick).
Oak.—FG, Blanda, 36.
Oak.—Miller, 12, pass from Lamonica (Blanda, kick).
Attendance—53,330.

INDIVIDUAL STATISTICS

Rushes—Oak: Dixon, 21 for 144 yards; Banaszak, 15 for 116; Lamonica, 5 for 22. Hou.: Granger, 14 for 19; Campbell, 6 for 15.
Passes—Oak.: Lamonica, 10 of 24 for 111 yards. Hou.: Beathard, 15 of 35 for 142.
Receptions—Oak.: Miller, 3 for 32; Cannon, 2 for 31; Biletnikoff, 2 for 19. Hou.: Frazier, 7 for 81; Campbell, 4 for 60.

TEAM STATISTICS

	Raiders	Oilers
First downs	18	11
Rushing yardage	263	38
Passing yardage	101	108
Return yardage	135	215
Passes	10-26	15-35
Interceptions by	1	0
Punts	4-44	11-39
Fumbles lost	0	2
Yards penalized	69	45

1967 NATIONAL LEAGUE CONFERENCE PLAYOFFS
WESTERN CONFERENCE
December 23 at Milwaukee
GREEN BAY PACKERS (28)

Offensive Ends—Dowler, Dale, Fleming, Long, McGee.
Defensive Ends—Davis, Aldridge, Brown.
Offensive Tackles—Gregg, Skoronski, Wright.
Defensive Tackles—Jordan, Kostelnik, Weatherwax.
Guards—Kramer, Gillingham, Thurston.
Centers—Bowman, Hyland.
Linebackers—Nitschke, Robinson, Caffey, Crutcher, Flanigan.
Quarterbacks—Starr, Bratkowski, Horn.
Running Backs—Anderson, Mercein, T. Williams, Wilson.
Defensive Backs—Adderley, Jeter, Wood, Brown, Hart, Rowser.
Kicker—Chandler.

LOS ANGELES RAMS (7)

Offensive Ends—Casey, Snow, Truax, Pope.
Defensive Ends—Jones, Lundy, Cajill.
Offensive Tackles—Cowan, Carollo, Nichols.
Defensive Tackles—Olsen, Brown, Talbert.
Guards—Mack, Scibelli, Chuy.
Centers—Iman, Burman.
Linebackers—Baughan, Pottios, Pardee, Woodlief, Guillory, Breen, Pivec.
Quarterbacks—Gabriel, Munson.
Running Backs—Bass, Josephson, Mason, Ellison.
Defensive Backs—Cross, C. Williams, Meador, Lamson, Crabb, Daniel, Winston.
Kickers—Kilgore, Gossett.

SCORING SUMMARY

Green Bay Packers	0	14	7	7—28
Los Angeles Rams	7	0	0	0— 7

L.A.—Casey, 29, pass from Gabriel (Gossett, kick).
G.B.—Williams, 47, run (Chandler, kick).
G.B.—Dale, 17, pass from Starr (Chandler, kick).
G.B.—Mercein, 6, run (Chandler, kick).
G.B.—T. Williams, 2, run (Chandler, kick).
Attendance—49,861.

INDIVIDUAL STATISTICS

Rushes—G.B.: T. Williams, 18 for 88 yards; Anderson, 12 for 52; Mercein, 12 for 13. L.A.: Bass, 14 for 40; Josephson, 9 for 16.
Passes—G.B.: Starr, 17 of 23 for 222 yards. L.A.: Gabriel, 11 of 31 for 186.
Receptions—G.B.: Dale, 6 for 109 yards; Dowler, 3 for 35; Fleming, 3 for 30. L.A.: Casey, 5 for 82; Truax, 2 for 45; Josephson, 2 for 30.

TEAM STATISTICS

	Packers	Rams
First downs	20	12
Rushing yardage	163	75
Passing yardage	211	142
Return yardage	83	104
Passes	17-23	11-31
Interceptions by	1	1
Punts	5-33	6-39
Fumbles lost	3	0
Yards penalized	44	25

EASTERN CONFERENCE
December 24 at Dallas
DALLAS COWBOYS (52)

Offensive Ends—Hayes, Rentzel, Norman, Clarke, Gent, Stokes.
Defensive Ends—Andrie, Stephens, East.
Offensive Tackles—Neely, Boeke, Wilbur.
Defensive Tackles—Lilly, Townes, Pugh.
Guards—Donohue, Liscio, Niland.
Centers—Connelly, Walker.
Linebackers—Jordan, Edwards, Howley, Hays, Tubbs.
Quarterbacks—Meredith, Morton, Rhome.
Running Backs—Perkins, Reeves, Baynham, Garrison, Shy.
Defensive Backs—Gaechter, Johnson, Renfro, C. Green, Clark, Daniels.
Kicker—Villanueva.

CLEVELAND BROWNS (14)

Offensive Ends—Collins, Warfield, Morin, Barney, McNeil, Smith.
Defensive Ends—Wiggin, Glass, Gregory.
Offensive Tackles—Schafrath, Clark, Demarie.
Defensive Tackles—Johnson, Kanicki, Parker.
Guards—Hickerson, Wooten, Taffoni, Copeland.
Center—Hoaglin.
Linebackers—Lindsey, Brewer, Houston, Matheson, Andrews.
Quarterbacks—Ryan, Lane.
Running Backs—Kelly, E. Green, Conjar, Pietrosante, Harraway.
Defensive Backs—Barnes, Howell, Fichtner, Kellerman, Ward, Davis.
Kicker—Groza.

SCORING SUMMARY

Dallas Cowboys	14	10	21	7—52
Cleveland Browns	0	7	0	7—14

Dal.—Baynham, 3, pass from Meredith (Villanueva, kick).
Dal.—Perkins, 4, run (Villanueva, kick).
Dal.—Hayes, 86, pass from Meredith (Villanueva, kick).
Dal.—FG, Villanueva, 10.
Cle.—Morin, 13, pass from Ryan (Groza, kick).
Dal.—Baynham, 1, run (Villanueva, kick).
Dal.—Perkins, 1, run (Villanueva, kick).
Dal.—C. Green, 60, interception (Villanueva, kick).
Dal.—Baynham, 1, run (Villanueva, kick).
Cle.—Warfield, 75, pass from Ryan (Groza, kick).
Attendance—70,786.

INDIVIDUAL STATISTICS

Rushes—Dal.: Perkins, 18 for 74 yards; Baynham, 13 for 50; Garrison, 9 for 33. Cle.: Kelly, 15 for 96; E. Green, 10 for 49.

Passes—Dal.: Meredith, 10 of 12 for 212; Morton, 1 of 3 for 13. Cle.: Ryan, 14 of 30 for 194.

Receptions—Dal.: Hayes, 5 for 144; Gent, 3 for 65. Cle.: Kelly, 4 for 39; Warfield, 3 for 99; Morin, 3 for 35; E. Green, 3 for 18.

TEAM STATISTICS

	Cowboys	Browns
First downs	22	15
Rushing yardage	178	159
Passing yardage	223	163
Return yardage	219	119
Passes	11-15	14-30
Interceptions by	1	1
Punts	2-44	7-40
Fumbles lost	1	0
Yards penalized	10	18

1967 FINAL STANDINGS

NATIONAL LEAGUE
Eastern Conference
Century Division

	W.	L.	T.	Pct.	Points For	Agt.
Cleveland	9	5	0	.643	334	297
New York	7	7	0	.500	369	379
St. Louis	6	7	1	.462	333	356
Pittsburgh	4	9	1	.308	281	320

Capitol Division

	W.	L.	T.	Pct.	For	Agt.
Dallas	9	5	0	.643	342	268
Philadelphia	6	7	1	.462	351	409
Washington	5	6	3	.455	347	353
New Orleans	3	11	0	.214	233	379

Western Conference
Central Division

	W.	L.	T.	Pct.	For	Agt.
Green Bay	9	4	1	.692	332	209
Chicago	7	6	1	.538	239	218
Detroit	5	7	2	.417	260	259
Minnesota	3	8	3	.273	233	294

Coastal Division

	W.	L.	T.	Pct.	For	Agt.
*Los Angeles	11	1	2	.917	398	196
Baltimore	11	1	2	.917	394	198
San Francisco	7	7	0	.500	273	337
Atlanta	1	12	1	.077	175	422

*Won division title by outscoring Baltimore in their two meetings.

AMERICAN LEAGUE
Eastern Division

	W.	L.	T.	Pct.	For	Agt.
Houston	9	4	1	.692	258	199
New York	8	5	1	.615	371	329
Buffalo	4	10	0	.286	237	285
Miami	4	10	0	.286	219	407
Boston	3	10	1	.231	280	389

Western Division

	W.	L.	T.	Pct.	For	Agt.
Oakland	13	1	0	.929	468	233
Kansas City	9	5	0	.643	408	254
San Diego	8	5	1	.615	360	352
Denver	3	11	0	.214	256	409

1967 NATIONAL LEAGUE SEASON RECORDS

Century Division

New York

37—St. Louis		20
24—Dallas		38
34—Washington		38
27—New Orleans		21
27—Pittsburgh		24
21—Green Bay		48
38—Cleveland		34
24—Minnesota		27
7—Chicago		34
28—Pittsburgh		20
44—Philadelphia		7
14—Cleveland		24
7—Detroit		30
37—St. Louis		14

Cleveland

14—Dallas		21
14—Detroit		31
42—New Orleans		7
21—Pittsburgh		10
20—St. Louis		16
24—Chicago		0
34—New York		38
34—Pittsburgh		14
7—Green Bay		55
14—Minnesota		10
42—Washington		37
24—New York		14
20—St. Louis		16
24—Philadelphia		28

Pittsburgh

41—Chicago		13
14—St. Louis		28
24—Philadelphia		34
10—Cleveland		21
24—New York		27
21—Dallas		24
14—New Orleans		10
14—Cleveland		34
14—St. Louis		14
20—New York		28
27—Minnesota		41
24—Detroit		14
10—Washington		15
24—Green Bay		17

St. Louis

20—New York		37
28—Pittsburgh		14
38—Detroit		28
34—Minnesota		24
16—Cleveland		20
48—Philadelphia		14
23—Green Bay		31
27—Washington		21
14—Pittsburgh		14
3—Chicago		30
21—Dallas		46
31—New Orleans		20
16—Cleveland		20
14—New York		37

Capitol Division

Dallas

21—Cleveland		14
38—New York		24
13—Los Angeles		35
17—Washington		14
14—New Orleans		10
24—Pittsburgh		21
14—Philadelphia		21
37—Atlanta		7
27—New Orleans		10
20—Washington		27
46—St. Louis		21
17—Baltimore		23
38—Philadelphia		17
16—San Francisco		24

New Orleans

13—Los Angeles		27
10—Washington		30
7—Cleveland		42
21—New York		27
10—Dallas		14
13—San Francisco		27
10—Pittsburgh		14
31—Philadelphia		24
10—Dallas		27
21—Philadelphia		48
27—Atlanta		24
20—St. Louis		31
10—Baltimore		30
30—Washington		14

Philadelphia

35—Washington		24
6—Baltimore		38
34—Pittsburgh		24
38—Atlanta		7
27—San Francisco		28
14—St. Louis		48
21—Dallas		14
24—New Orleans		31
17—Los Angeles		33
48—New Orleans		21
7—New York		44
35—Washington		35
17—Dallas		38
28—Cleveland		24

Washington

24—Philadelphia		35
30—New Orleans		10
38—New York		34
14—Dallas		17
20—Atlanta		20
28—Los Angeles		28
13—Baltimore		17
21—St. Louis		27
31—San Francisco		28
27—Dallas		20
37—Cleveland		42
35—Philadelphia		35
15—Pittsburgh		10
14—New Orleans		30

Central Division

Chicago
13—Pittsburgh _____ 41
10—Green Bay _____ 13
17—Minnesota _____ 7
3—Baltimore _____ 24
14—Detroit _____ 3
0—Cleveland _____ 24
17—Los Angeles _____ 28
27—Detroit _____ 13
34—New York _____ 7
30—St. Louis _____ 3
13—Green Bay _____ 17
28—San Francisco _____ 14
10—Minnesota _____ 10
23—Atlanta _____ 14

Green Bay
17—Detroit _____ 17
13—Chicago _____ 10
23—Atlanta _____ 0
27—Detroit _____ 17
7—Minnesota _____ 10
48—New York _____ 21
31—St. Louis _____ 23
10—Baltimore _____ 13
55—Cleveland _____ 7
13—San Francisco _____ 0
17—Chicago _____ 13
30—Minnesota _____ 27
24—Los Angeles _____ 27
17—Pittsburgh _____ 24

Detroit
17—Green Bay _____ 17
31—Cleveland _____ 14
28—St. Louis _____ 38
17—Green Bay _____ 27
3—Chicago _____ 14
24—Atlanta _____ 3
45—San Francisco _____ 3
13—Chicago _____ 27
10—Minnesota _____ 10
7—Baltimore _____ 41
7—Los Angeles _____ 31
14—Pittsburgh _____ 24
30—New York _____ 7
14—Minnesota _____ 3

Minnesota
21—San Francisco _____ 27
3—Los Angeles _____ 39
7—Chicago _____ 17
24—St. Louis _____ 34
10—Green Bay _____ 7
20—Baltimore _____ 20
20—Atlanta _____ 21
27—New York _____ 24
10—Detroit _____ 10
10—Cleveland _____ 14
41—Pittsburgh _____ 27
27—Green Bay _____ 30
10—Chicago _____ 10
3—Detroit _____ 14

Coastal Division

Atlanta
31—Baltimore _____ 38
7—San Francisco _____ 38
0—Green Bay _____ 23
7—Philadelphia _____ 38
20—Washington _____ 20
3—Detroit _____ 24
21—Minnesota _____ 20
7—Dallas _____ 37
7—Baltimore _____ 49
3—Los Angeles _____ 31
24—New Orleans _____ 27
3—Los Angeles _____ 20
28—San Francisco _____ 34
14—Chicago _____ 23

Los Angeles
27—New Orleans _____ 13
39—Minnesota _____ 3
35—Dallas _____ 13
24—San Francisco _____ 27
24—Baltimore _____ 24
28—Washington _____ 28
28—Chicago _____ 17
17—San Francisco _____ 7
33—Philadelphia _____ 28
31—Atlanta _____ 3
31—Detroit _____ 7
20—Atlanta _____ 3
27—Green Bay _____ 24
34—Baltimore _____ 10

Baltimore
38—Atlanta _____ 31
38—Philadelphia _____ 6
41—San Francisco _____ 7
24—Chicago _____ 3
24—Los Angeles _____ 24
20—Minnesota _____ 20
17—Washington _____ 13
13—Green Bay _____ 10
49—Atlanta _____ 7
41—Detroit _____ 7
26—San Francisco _____ 9
23—Dallas _____ 17
30—New Orleans _____ 10
10—Los Angeles _____ 34

San Francisco
27—Minnesota _____ 21
38—Atlanta _____ 7
7—Baltimore _____ 41
27—Los Angeles _____ 24
28—Philadelphia _____ 27
27—New Orleans _____ 13
3—Detroit _____ 45
7—Los Angeles _____ 17
28—Washington _____ 31
0—Green Bay _____ 13
9—Baltimore _____ 26
14—Chicago _____ 28
34—Atlanta _____ 28
24—Dallas _____ 16

1967 AMERICAN LEAGUE SEASON RECORDS

Eastern Division

New York
17—Buffalo	20
38—Denver	24
29—Miami	7
27—Oakland	14
28—Houston	28
33—Miami	14
30—Boston	23
18—Kansas City	42
20—Buffalo	10
29—Boston	24
24—Denver	33
7—Kansas City	21
29—Oakland	38
42—San Diego	31

Houston
20—Kansas City	25
20—Buffalo	3
3—San Diego	13
10—Denver	6
28—New York	28
24—Kansas City	19
10—Buffalo	3
7—Boston	18
20—Denver	18
27—Boston	6
17—Miami	14
7—Oakland	19
24—San Diego	17
41—Miami	10

Boston
21—Denver	26
14—San Diego	28
7—Oakland	35
23—Buffalo	0
31—San Diego	31
41—Miami	10
48—Oakland	14
23—New York	30
18—Houston	7
10—Kansas City	33
24—New York	29
6—Houston	27
16—Buffalo	44
32—Miami	41

Buffalo
20—New York	17
3—Houston	20
0—Boston	23
17—San Diego	37
17—Denver	16
20—Oakland	24
3—Houston	10
35—Miami	13
10—New York	20
20—Denver	21
14—Miami	17
13—Kansas City	23
44—Boston	16
21—Oakland	28

Miami
35—Denver	21
0—Kansas City	24
7—New York	29
0—Kansas City	41
10—Boston	41
14—New York	33
13—Buffalo	35

Miami
0—San Diego	24
17—Oakland	31
17—Buffalo	14
14—Houston	17
41—San Diego	24
41—Boston	32
10—Houston	41

Western Division

Denver
26—Boston	21
0—Oakland	51
21—Miami	35
24—New York	38
6—Houston	10
16—Buffalo	17
21—San Diego	38
9—Kansas City	52
17—Oakland	21
18—Houston	20
21—Buffalo	20
20—San Diego	24
33—New York	24
24—Kansas City	38

Oakland
51—Denver	0
35—Boston	7
23—Kansas City	21
14—New York	27
24—Buffalo	20
48—Boston	14
51—San Diego	10
21—Denver	17
31—Miami	17
44—Kansas City	22
41—San Diego	21
19—Houston	7
38—New York	29
28—Buffalo	21

Kansas City		San Diego	
25—Houston	20	28—Boston	14
24—Miami	0	13—Houston	3
21—Oakland	23	37—Buffalo	17
41—Miami	0	31—Boston	31
31—San Diego	45	45—Kansas City	31
19—Houston	24	38—Denver	21
52—Denver	9	10—Oakland	51
42—New York	18	24—Miami	0
33—Boston	10	17—Kansas City	16
16—San Diego	17	24—Denver	20
22—Oakland	44	21—Oakland	41
23—Buffalo	13	24—Miami	41
21—New York	7	17—Houston	24
38—Denver	24	31—New York	42

1967 ALL-STAR TEAMS

NATIONAL LEAGUE

Associated Press
First Team

OFFENSE
SE—Charlie Taylor, Washington
TE—John Mackey, Baltimore
T—Ralph Neely, Dallas
T—Forrest Gregg, Green Bay
G—Jerry Kramer, Green Bay
G—Gene Hickerson, Cleveland
C—Bob DeMarco, St. Louis
Q—Johnny Unitas, Baltimore
B—Gale Sayers, Chicago
B—Leroy Kelly, Cleveland
FL—Willie Richardson, Baltimore

DEFENSE
E—Deacon Jones, Los Angeles
E—Willie Davis, Green Bay
T—Merlin Olsen, Los Angeles
T—Bob Lilly, Dallas
ML—Tommy Nobis, Atlanta
OL—Dave Robinson, Green Bay
OL—Chuck Howley, Dallas
CB—Bob Jeter, Green Bay
CB—Cornell Green, Dallas
S—Willie Wood, Green Bay
S—Larry Wilson, St. Louis

Second Team

OFFENSE
SE—Homer Jones, New York
TE—Jerry Smith, Washington
T—Bob Brown, Philadelphia
T—Ernie McMillan, St. Louis
G—John Gordy, Detroit
G—Ken Gray, St. Louis
C—Mick Tinglehoff, Minnesota
Q—Sonny Jurgensen, Washington
B—Johnny Roland, St. Louis
B—Don Perkins, Dallas
FL—Bob Hayes, Dallas

DEFENSE
E—Ordell Braase, Baltimore
E—George Andrie, Dallas
T—Alex Karras, Detroit
T—Chuck Walker, St. Louis
ML—Ray Nitschke, Green Bay
OL—Maxie Baughan, Los Angeles
OL—Dave Wilcox, San Francisco
CB—Herb Adderley, Green Bay
CB—Dave Whitsell, New Orleans
S—Eddie Meador, Los Angeles
S—Richie Petitbon, Chicago

United Press International
First Team

OFFENSE
SE—Charlie Taylor, Washington
TE—Jackie Smith, St. Louis
T—Ralph Neely, Dallas
T—Forrest Gregg, Green Bay
G—Jerry Kramer, Green Bay
G—Gene Hickerson, Cleveland
C—Mick Tinglehoff, Minnesota
Q—Johnny Unitas, Baltimore
B—Gale Sayers, Chicago
B—Leroy Kelly, Cleveland
FL—Homer Jones, New York

DEFENSE
E—Deacon Jones, Los Angeles
E—Willie Davis, Green Bay
T—Merlin Olsen, Los Angeles
T—Bob Lilly, Dallas
ML—Dick Butkus, Chicago
OL—Dave Robinson, Green Bay
OL—Maxie Baughan, Los Angeles
CB—Bob Jeter, Green Bay
CB—Cornell Green, Dallas
S—Willie Wood, Green Bay
S—Eddie Meador, Los Angeles

Second Team

OFFENSE
SE—Willie Richardson, Baltimore
TE—John Mackey, Baltimore
T—Bob Brown, Philadelphia
T—Charlie Cowan, Los Angeles
G—John Gordy, Detroit
G—Ken Gray, St. Louis
C—Bob DeMarco, St. Louis
Q—Sonny Jurgensen, Washington
B—Johnny Roland, St. Louis
B—Dave Osborn, Minnesota
FL—Bob Hayes, Dallas

DEFENSE
E—Ordell Braase, Baltimore
E—Carl Eller, Minnesota
T—Alex Karras, Detroit
T—Chuck Walker, St. Louis
ML—Tommy Nobis, Atlanta
OL—Chuck Howley, Dallas
OL—Dave Wilcox, San Francisco
CB—Bob Boyd, Baltimore
CB—Dave Whitsell, New Orleans
S—Larry Wilson, St. Louis
S—Richie Petitbon, Chicago

AMERICAN LEAGUE

Associated Press
First Team

OFFENSE
SE—George Sauer, New York
TE—Billy Cannon, Oakland
T—Jim Tyrer, Kansas City
T—Ron Mix, San Diego
G—Walt Sweeney, San Diego
G—Bob Talamini, Houston
C—Jim Otto, Oakland
Q—Daryle Lamonica, Oakland
B—Mike Garrett, Kansas City
B—Jim Nance, Boston
FL—Lance Alworth, San Diego

DEFENSE
E—Pat Holmes, Houston
E—Ben Davidson, Oakland
T—Tom Keating, Oakland
T—Buck Buchanan, Kansas City
ML—Nick Buoniconti, Boston
OL—George Webster, Houston
OL—Bobby Bell, Kansas City
CB—Miller Farr, Houston
CB—Kent McCloughan, Oakland
S—George Saimes, Buffalo
S—Johnny Robinson, Kansas City

Second Team

OFFENSE
SE—Al Denson, Denver
TE—Fred Arbanas, Kansas City
T—Harry Schuh, Oakland
T—Walt Suggs, Houston
G—Ed Budde, Kansas City
G—Wayne Hawkins, Oakland
C—Bobby Maples, Houston
Q—Joe Namath, New York
B—Hewritt Dixon, Oakland
B—Hoyle Granger, Houston
FL—Don Maynard, New York

DEFENSE
E—Ron McDole, Buffalo
E—Jerry Mays, Kansas City
T—Dave Costa, Denver
T—Houston Antwine, Boston
ML—Dan Conners, Oakland
OL—Larry Grantham, New York
OL—Mike Stratton, Buffalo
CB—Les Duncan, San Diego
CB—Willie Brown, Oakland
S—Jim Norton, Houston
S—Rodger Bird, Oakland

United Press International
First Team

OFFENSE
SE—George Sauer, New York
TE—Billy Cannon, Oakland
T—Ron Mix, San Diego
T—Harry Schuh, Oakland
G—Walt Sweeney, San Diego
G—Bob Talamini, Houston
C—Jim Otto, Oakland
Q—Daryle Lamonica, Oakland
FL—Lance Alworth, San Diego
H—Mike Garrett, Kansas City
F—Jim Nance, Boston

DEFENSE
E—Ben Davidson, Oakland
E—Pat Holmes, Houston
T—Tom Keating, Oakland
T—Buck Buchanan, Kansas City
ML—Nick Buoniconti, Boston
OL—George Webster, Houston
OL—Bobby Bell, Kansas City
CB—Miller Farr, Houston
CB—Kent McCloughan, Oakland
S—Johnny Robinson, Kansas City
S—George Saimes, Buffalo

Second Team

OFFENSE	DEFENSE
SE—Al Denson, Denver	E—Gerry Philbin, New York
TE—Fred Arbanas, Kansas City	E—Ron McDole, Buffalo
T—Jim Tyrer, Kansas City	T—Houston Antwine, Boston
T—Walt Suggs, Houston	T—Dave Costa, Denver
G—Gene Upshaw, Oakland	ML—Dan Conners, Oakland
G—Wayne Hawkins, Oakland	OL—Frank Buncom, San Diego
C—Bobby Maples, Houston	OL—Gus Otto, Oakland
Q—Joe Namath, New York	CB—Dick Westmoreland, Miami
FL—Don Maynard, New York	CB—Willie Brown, Oakland
H—Hoyle Granger, Houston	S—Jim Norton, Houston
F—Hewritt Dixon, Oakland	S—Kenny Graham, San Diego

NFL STATISTICS FOR 1967

1967 PASSING—INDIVIDUAL

	Std.	Att.	Comp.	Pct. Comp.	Yds. Gain	Tds	Long	Had Int.	Pct. Int.	Avg. Gain
Jurgensen, Wash.	1	*508	*288	56.7	*3747	*31	t86	16	*3.1	7.38
Unitas, Balt.	2	436	255	*58.5	3428	20	t88	16	3.7	7.86
Tarkenton, N. Y.	3	377	204	54.1	3088	29	t70	19	5.0	8.19
Gabriel, L. A.	4	371	196	52.8	2779	25	t80	13	3.5	7.49
Snead, Phil.	5	434	240	55.3	3399	29	t87	24	5.5	7.83
†Starr, G. B.	6	210	115	54.8	1823	9	84	17	8.1	*8.68
Ryan, Clev.	7	280	136	48.6	2026	20	t49	16	5.7	7.24
Meredith, Dall.	8	255	128	50.2	1834	16	t60	16	6.3	7.19
Cuozzo, N. O.	9	260	134	51.5	1562	7	t49	12	4.6	6.01
Hart, St. L.	10	397	192	48.4	3008	19	t76	30	7.6	7.58
Brodie, S. F.	11	349	168	48.1	2013	11	t63	16	4.6	5.77
Nelsen, Pitt.	12	165	74	44.8	1125	10	t58	9	5.5	6.82
Nix, Pitts.	13	268	136	50.7	1587	8	t66	19	7.1	5.92
Plum, Det.	14	172	86	50.0	925	4	43	*8	4.7	5.38
Kilmer, N. O.	15	204	97	47.5	1341	6	*96	11	5.4	6.57
Johnson, Atl.	16	288	142	49.3	1620	10	t82	21	7.3	5.63
Concannon, Chi.	17	186	92	49.5	1260	6	t93	14	7.5	6.77
Sweetan, Det.	18	177	74	41.8	901	10	t52	11	6.2	5.09
Kapp, Minn.	19	214	102	47.7	1386	8	t85	17	7.9	6.48
Morton, Dall.	—	137	69	50.4	987	10	t64	10	7.3	7.14
Bratkowski, G. B.	—	94	53	56.4	724	5	t86	9	9.6	7.70
VanderKelen, Minn.	—	115	45	39.1	522	3	42	7	6.1	4.54
Mira, S. F.	—	65	35	53.8	592	5	58	3	4.6	9.11
Nofsinger, Atl.	—	60	30	50.0	352	1	38	2	3.3	5.87
Spurrier, S. F.	—	50	23	46.0	211	0	21	7	14.0	4.22
Lane, Clev.	—	43	21	48.8	254	2	23	1	2.3	5.91
Rakestraw, Chi.	—	44	21	47.7	228	3	34	2	4.5	5.18
Bukich, Chi.	—	33	18	54.5	185	0	30	2	6.1	5.61
Morrall, N. Y.	—	24	13	54.2	181	3	t27	1	4.2	7.54
Ninowski, Wash.	—	18	12	66.7	123	0	31	1	5.6	6.83
Horn, G. B.	—	24	12	50.0	171	1	t29	1	4.2	7.13
Johnson, S. L.	—	29	12	41.4	162	1	t36	3	10.3	5.59

	Std.	Att.	Comp.	Pct. Comp.	Yds. Gain	Tds	Long	Had Int.	Pct. Int.	Avg. Gain
Ward, Balt.	—	16	9	56.3	115	2	t21	1	6.3	7.19
Rhome, Dall.	—	18	9	50.0	86	0	19	1	5.6	4.78
Munson, L. A.	—	10	5	50.0	38	1	18	2	20.0	3.80
Wood, N. O.	—	11	5	45.5	62	0	27	0	0.0	5.64
Reeves, Dall.	—	7	4	57.1	195	2	t74	1	14.3	27.86
Hoak, Pitt.	—	8	4	50.0	69	1	21	1	12.5	8.63
Sloan, Atl.	—	18	4	22.2	38	0	15	2	11.1	2.11
Koy, N. Y.	—	4	3	75.0	101	1	t68	0	0.0	25.25
Berry, Minn.	—	7	3	42.9	43	0	21	0	0.0	6.14
Shiner, Clev.	—	9	3	33.3	34	0	21	1	11.1	3.78

Moore, Atl.	2	2	100.0	102	1	t75	0	0.0	51.00
Mason, L. A.	3	2	66.7	65	1	t51	0	0.0	21.67
Crow, S. F.	5	2	40.0	46	0	25	0	0.0	9.20
Josephson, L. A.	5	2	40.0	47	0	24	1	20.0	9.40
K. Hill, Phil.	7	2	28.6	33	1	18	0	0.0	4.71
Lang, Phil.	1	1	100.0	26	0	26	0	0.0	26.00
McNeill, N. O.	1	1	100.0	24	0	24	0	0.0	24.00
Meador, L. A.	1	1	100.0	18	1	t18	0	0.0	18.00
Mitchell, Wash.	1	1	100.0	17	0	17	0	0.0	17.00
Morrison, N. Y.	1	1	100.0	12	0	12	0	0.0	12.00
Pitts, G. B.	1	1	100.0	21	0	21	0	0.0	21.00
Dunn, Atl.	2	1	50.0	32	1	t32	0	0.0	16.00
Anderson, G. B.	2	1	50.0	19	0	19	0	0.0	9.50
Dial, Phil.	3	1	33.3	5	0	5	0	0.0	1.67
Matte, Balt.	5	1	20.0	18	0	18	0	0.0	3.60
Clark, Pitt.	1	0	00.0	0	0	0	0	0.0	0.00
Kelly, Clev.	1	0	00.0	0	0	0	0	0.0	0.00
Smith, St. L.	1	0	00.0	0	0	0	1	100.0	0.00
Barrington, N. O.	2	0	00.0	0	0	0	0	0.0	0.00
Farr, Det.	2	0	00.0	0	0	0	0	0.0	0.00
Roland, St. L.	4	0	00.0	0	0	0	1	25.0	0.00
Sayers, Chi.	5	0	00.0	0	0	0	0	0.0	0.00

*—High for 1967.
†—1966 Leader.
t—Touchdown.

NOTE: Standing based on percent of completions, touchdown passes, percent of interceptions and average yards gained. To qualify for championship rating a player must throw at least 140 passes.

1967 PUNT RETURNS—INDIVIDUAL

	Stdg.	No.	F.C.	Yards	Avg.	Long	Tds.
DAVIS, CLEV.	1	18	7	229	*12.7	t52	*1
Hayes, Dall.	2	24	6	*276	11.5	t69	*1
Cunningham, S. F.	3	*27	7	249	9.2	57	0
Harris, Wash.	4	23	12	208	9.0	51	0
Spiller, St. L.	5	15	*13	124	8.3	33	0
Cross, L. A.	6	17	6	136	8.0	39	0
Martin, Phil.	7	20	4	128	6.4	30	0
Meador, L. A.	8	21	7	131	6.2	22	0
Bradshaw, Pitt.	9	16	*13	97	6.1	26	0
Haymond, Balt.	10	26	4	155	6.0	32	0
Smith, Atl.	11	20	2	92	4.6	26	0
Grim, Minn.	12	25	10	101	4.0	*81	0
Watkins, Det.	13	15	3	57	3.8	18	0
Gordon, Chi.		12	12	82	6.8	43	0
Wood, G. B.		12	6	3	0.3	8	0
Volk, Balt.		11	4	88	8.0	24	0
Roberts, N. O.		11	12	50	4.5	11	0
Love, Wash.		11	5	—5	—0.5	7	0
Anderson, G. B.		9	3	98	10.9	43	0
Kelly, Clev.		9	4	59	6.6	32	0
T. Brown, G. B.		9	1	40	4.4	12	0
Shivers, St. L.		9	5	36	4.0	31	0
Thomas, Pitt.		9	2	34	3.8	17	0
Thompson, Det.		9	9	20	2.2	7	0
Pitts, G. B.		9	3	16	1.8	10	0
Lockhart, N. Y.		7	7	54	7.7	19	0
Gilliam, N. O.		7	6	13	1.9	8	0
Keys, Pitt.-Minn.		7	9	7	1.0	8	0
Alexander, S. F.		6	1	64	10.7	31	0
Ward, Clev.		6	3	62	10.3	24	0
Rentzel, Dall.		6	8	45	7.5	21	0
Tucker, L. A.		6	1	40	6.7	11	0
Williams, N. Y.		6	4	28	4.7	7	0
Latourette, St. L.		6	4	21	3.5	17	0
Logan, Balt.		5	2	80	16.0	t43	*1
Morris, Chi.		4	4	24	6.0	15	0
Barney, Det.		4	8	14	3.5	6	0

	Stdg.	No.	F.C.	Yards	Avg.	Long	Tds.
Minnlear, N. Y.	—	4	0	13	3.3	5	0
Stiger, L. A.	—	4	0	9	2.3	5	0
Vaughn, Det.	—	4	4	7	1.8	12	0
Sharockman, Minn.	—	4	6	0	0.0	3	0
Sayers, Chi.	—	3	8	80	26.7	t58	*1
†Roland, St. L.	—	3	8	17	5.7	11	0
Shann, Phil.	—	3	2	17	5.7	8	0
Hughes, Phil.	—	3	0	11	3.7	11	0
Dodd, Chi.	—	3	4	8	2.7	6	0
Hathcock, N. Y.	—	3	2	7	2.3	7	0
Brown, N. O.	—	3	2	1	0.3	13	0
Simmons, Atl.	—	3	1	0	0.0	0	0
Renfro, Dall.	—	3	4	—1	-0.3	7	0
Douglas, N. O.	—	2	1	15	7.5	12	0
Fitzgerald, Minn.-Atl.	—	2	1	4	2.0	4	0
Harris, N. Y.	—	2	1	0	0.0	0	0
Winston, L. A.	—	1	0	12	12.0	12	0
Jefferson, Pitt.	—	1	0	10	10.0	10	0
Harraway, Clev.	—	1	0	7	7.0	7	0
Hudlow, Atl.	—	1	2	2	2.0	2	0
Marion, Pitt.	—	1	2	2	2.0	2	0
Scarpati, Phil.	—	1	2	2	2.0	2	0
Tucker, S. F.	—	1	0	1	1.0	1	0
Crabb, L. A.	—	1	0	0	0.0	0	0
Gonsoulin, S. F.	—	1	0	0	0.0	0	0
Lince, Phil.	—	1	0	0	0.0	0	0
Reed, Phil.	—	1	0	0	0.0	0	0
Weger, Det.	—	1	0	0	0.0	0	0
C. Williams, St. L.	—	1	0	0	0.0	0	0
Youngblood, Clev.	—	1	0	0	0.0	0	0
Felts, L. A.	—	1	0	—1	-1.0	—1	0
Shy, Pitt	—	1	1	—5	-5.0	—5	0
Lewis, S. F.	—	0	1	0	0.0	0	0
Medved, Phil.	—	0	1	0	0.0	0	0
Rassas, Atl.	—	0	1	0	0.0	0	0
Reaves, Atl.	—	0	1	0	0.0	0	0
Taylor, Wash.	—	0	3	0	0.0	0	0

*—High for 1967.
†—1966 Leader.
t—Touchdown.
NOTE: Standing based on average return. To qualify for championship rating
a player must return at least 14 punts.

1967 SCORING—INDIVIDUAL

	Td. R.	Td. P.	Td. Rb.	Tot. Tds.	XP	XPM	FG	FGA	Tot. Pts.
BAKKEN, S. L.	0	0	0	0	36	0	*27	39	*117
†Gossett, L. A.	0	0	0	0	*48	2	20	*43	108
Michaels, Balt.	0	0	0	0	46	2	20	37	106
Chandler, G. B.	0	0	0	0	39	0	19	29	96
Jones, N. Y.	1	*13	0	*14	0	0	0	0	84
Baker, Phil.	0	0	0	0	45	0	12	19	81
Kelly, Clev.	*11	2	0	13	0	0	0	0	78
Cox, Minn.	0	0	0	0	26	0	17	33	77
Groza, Clev.	0	0	0	0	43	0	11	23	76
Davis, S. F.	0	0	0	0	33	0	14	33	75
Matte, Balt.	9	3	0	12	0	0	0	0	72
Sayers, Chi.	7	1	*4	12	0	0	0	0	72
J. Smith, Wash.	0	12	0	12	0	0	0	0	72
Clark, Pitt.	0	0	0	0	35	0	12	22	71
Durkee, N. O.	0	0	0	0	27	0	14	32	69
Hayes, Dall.	0	10	1	11	0	0	0	0	66
Reeves, Dall.	5	6	0	11	0	0	0	0	66
Roland, St. L.	10	1	0	11	0	0	0	0	66
Percival, Chi.	0	0	0	0	26	*3	13	26	65
Hawkins, Phil.	0	10	0	10	0	0	0	0	60

Player									
Woodeshick, Phil.	6	4	0	10	0	0	0	0	60
Villanueva, Dall.	0	0	0	0	32	2	8	19	56
Anderson, G. B.	6	3	0	9	0	0	0	0	54
Morrison, N. Y.	2	7	0	9	0	0	0	0	54
Smith, St. L.	0	9	0	9	0	0	0	0	54
Taylor, Wash.	0	9	0	9	0	0	0	0	54
Thomas, N. Y.	0	9	0	9	0	0	0	0	54
Casey, L. A.	0	8	0	8	0	0	0	0	48
Josephson, L. A.	4	4	0	8	0	0	0	0	48
Rentzel, Dall.	0	8	0	8	0	0	0	0	48
Richardson, Balt.	0	8	0	8	0	0	0	0	48
Snow, L. A.	0	8	0	8	0	0	0	0	48
Warfield, Clev.	0	8	0	8	0	0	0	0	48
Gogolak, N. Y.	0	0	0	0	28	1	6	10	46
Traynham, Atl.	0	0	0	0	22	0	7	18	43
Ballman, Phil.	1	6	0	7	0	0	0	0	42
Bass, L. A.	6	1	0	7	0	0	0	0	42
Collins, Clev.	0	7	0	7	0	0	0	0	42
Lewis, S. F.	6	1	0	7	0	0	0	0	42
Mitchell, Wash.	1	6	0	7	0	0	0	0	42
Abramowicz, N. O.	0	6	0	6	0	0	0	0	36
Farr, Det.	3	3	0	6	0	0	0	0	36
Gabriel, L. A.	6	0	0	6	0	0	0	0	36
E. Green, Clev.	4	2	0	6	0	0	0	0	36
Lorick, Balt.	6	0	0	6	0	0	0	0	36
Nowatzke, Det.	4	2	0	6	0	0	0	0	36
Perkins, Dall.	6	0	0	6	0	0	0	0	36
Pitts, G. B.	6	0	0	6	0	0	0	0	36
Willard, S. F.	5	1	0	6	0	0	0	0	36
Williams, G. B.	1	6	*4	6	0	0	0	0	36
Love, Wash.	0	1	2	3	10	1	2	7	34
Mingo, Wash.	0	0	0	0	20	2	4	10	32
Brown, Minn.	5	0	0	5	0	0	0	0	30
Coffey, Atl.	4	1	0	5	0	0	0	0	30
Crow, S. F.	2	3	0	5	0	0	0	0	30
Dale, G. B.	0	5	0	5	0	0	0	0	30
Gordon, Chi.	0	5	0	5	0	0	0	0	30
Hilton, Pitt.	0	5	0	5	0	0	0	0	30
Koy, N. Y.	4	1	0	5	0	0	0	0	30
Lang, Phil.	2	3	0	5	0	0	0	0	30
Roberts, N. O.	0	3	2	5	0	0	0	0	30
Shy, Pitt.	4	1	0	5	0	0	0	0	30
Watkins, Det.	4	1	0	5	0	0	0	0	30
Wilburn, Pitt.	0	5	0	5	0	0	0	0	30
D. Williams, St. L.	0	5	0	5	0	0	0	0	30
Yepremian, Det.	0	0	0	0	22	1	2	6	28
Walker, Det.	0	0	0	0	11	0	5	15	26
Murdock, N. Y.	0	0	0	0	13	2	4	9	25
Allen, Wash.	3	1	0	4	0	0	0	0	24
Asbury, Pitt.	4	0	0	4	0	0	0	0	24
Beasley, Minn.	0	4	0	4	0	0	0	0	24
Dowler, G. B.	0	4	0	4	0	0	0	0	24
Hawkins, Balt.	0	4	0	4	0	0	0	0	24
Jefferson, Pitt.	0	4	0	4	0	0	0	0	24
Kelly, Phil.	0	4	0	4	0	0	0	0	24
Malinchak, Det.	0	4	0	4	0	0	0	0	24
McDonald, Wash.	4	0	0	4	0	0	0	0	24
McDonald, Atl.	0	4	0	4	0	0	0	0	24
Moore, Balt.	4	0	0	4	0	0	0	0	24
Randle, S. F.	0	4	0	4	0	0	0	0	24
Truax, L. A.	0	4	0	4	0	0	0	0	24
Barney, Det.	0	0	3	3	0	0	0	0	18
Concannon, Chi.	3	0	0	3	0	0	0	0	18
Grabowski, G. B.	2	1	0	3	0	0	0	0	18
Hart, S. L.	3	0	0	3	0	0	0	0	18
Mackey, Balt.	0	3	0	3	0	0	0	0	18
Marsh, Det.	2	1	0	3	0	0	0	0	18
Martin, Atl.	0	3	0	3	0	0	0	0	18
Osborn, Minn.	2	1	0	3	0	0	0	0	18
Phillips, Minn.	0	3	0	3	0	0	0	0	18

	Td. R.	Td. P.	Td. Rb.	Tot. Tds.	XP	XPM	FG	FGA	Tot. Pts.
Whitfield, Wash.	1	2	0	3	0	0	0	0	18
Windsor, S. F.	0	2	1	3	0	0	0	0	18
Witcher, S. F.	0	3	0	3	0	0	0	0	18
Anderson, Pitt.	0	2	0	2	0	0	0	0	12
Brown, N. O.	2	0	0	2	0	0	0	0	12
T. Brown, Phil.	1	1	0	2	0	0	0	0	12
Clarke, Dall.	1	1	0	2	0	0	0	0	12
Conrad, St. L.	0	2	0	2	0	0	0	0	12
Cunningham, S. F.	2	0	0	2	0	0	0	0	12
Deters, Dall.	0	0	0	0	9	1	1	4	12
Ditka, Phil.	0	2	0	2	0	0	0	0	12

	Td. R.	Td. P.	Td. Rb.	Tot. Tds.	XP	XPM	FG	FGA	Tot. Pts.
Frederickson, N. Y.	2	0	0	2	0	0	0	0	12
Gambrell, St. L.	0	2	0	2	0	0	0	0	12
Gautt, St. L.	1	1	0	2	0	0	0	0	12
Gilliam, N. O.	0	1	1	2	0	0	0	0	12
Hand, Det.	0	0	2	2	0	0	0	0	12
Hill, Balt.	2	0	0	2	0	0	0	0	12
Hoak, Pitt.	1	1	0	2	0	0	0	0	12
Houston, Clev.	0	0	2	2	0	0	0	0	12
Jurgensen, Wash.	2	0	0	2	0	0	0	0	12
Kapp, Minn.	2	0	0	2	0	0	0	0	12
Kramer, N. O.	0	2	0	2	0	0	0	0	12
Mackbee, Minn.	0	0	2	2	0	0	0	0	12
McCall, N. O.	1	1	0	2	0	0	0	0	12
McNeil, Clev.	0	2	0	2	0	0	0	0	12
B. McRae, Chi.	0	0	2	2	0	0	0	0	12
Meador, L. A.	0	0	2	2	0	0	0	0	12
Minniear, N. Y.	1	1	0	2	0	0	0	0	12
Nix, Pitt.	2	0	0	2	0	0	0	0	12
Norman, Dall.	0	2	0	2	0	0	0	0	12
Pardee, L. A.	0	2	0	2	0	0	0	0	12
Parks, S. F.	0	2	0	2	0	0	0	0	12
Perkins, Balt.	0	2	0	2	0	0	0	0	12
Pope, L. A.	0	2	0	2	0	0	0	0	12
Rakestraw, Chi.	2	0	0	2	0	0	0	0	12
Schultz, N. O.	2	0	0	2	0	0	0	0	12
Simmons, Atl.	0	2	0	2	0	0	0	0	12
Smith, Clev.	0	1	1	2	0	0	0	0	12
Snead, Phil.	2	0	0	2	0	0	0	0	12
Studstill, Det.	0	2	0	2	0	0	0	0	12
Tarkenton, N. Y.	2	0	0	2	0	0	0	0	12
Taylor, N. O.	2	0	0	2	0	0	0	0	12
Triplett, N. Y.	2	0	0	2	0	0	0	0	12
Washington, Minn.	0	2	0	2	0	0	0	0	12
Wilson, G. B.	2	0	0	2	0	0	0	0	12
Whitsell, N. O.	0	0	2	2	0	0	0	0	12

*—High for 1967.
†—1966 Leader.

SAFETIES SCORED BY: Jordan & Pugh, Dall.; Maher, Det.; Davis, G. B.; Jones, L. A.; Anderson, N. O.; Breding, Wash.

1967 INTERCEPTIONS—INDIVIDUAL

	No.	Yds.	Avg.	Long	Tds.
BARNEY, DET.	*10	*232	23.2	t71	*3
WHITSELL, N. O.	*10	178	17.8	t41	2
Meador, L. A.	8	103	12.9	t30	2
Jeter, G. B.	8	78	9.8	25	0
Krause, Wash.	8	75	9.4	32	0
Reaves, Atl.	7	153	21.9	42	0
Green, Dall.	7	52	7.4	28	0
Woodson, Pitt.	7	49	7.0	24	0
Renfro, Dall.	7	38	5.4	30	0
Boyd, Balt.	6	145	24.2	41	1

	No.	Yds.	Avg.	Long	Tds.
Volk, Balt.	6	145	24.2	*†94	1
Pardee, L. A.	6	95	15.8	t40	2
Mackbee, Minn.	5	98	19.6	40	1
B. McRae, Chi.	5	94	18.8	t34	2
Johnson, Dall.	5	88	17.6	49	0
Petitbon, Chi.	5	73	14.6	35	0
Alexander, S. F.	5	72	14.4	48	0
Lyles, Balt.	5	59	11.8	t36	1
Lockhart, N. Y.	5	38	7.6	28	0
R. Taylor, Chi.	5	19	3.8	10	0
Fichtner, Clev.	4	113	28.3	88	0
Scarpati, Phil.	4	99	24.8	t67	1
Fischer, St. L.	4	85	21.3	t69	1
Williams, L. A.	4	75	18.8	29	0
†Wilson, St. L.	4	75	18.8	44	0
Baughan, L. A.	4	69	17.3	31	0
Wood, G. B.	4	60	15.0	25	0
Costello, N. Y.	4	54	13.5	26	0
Nettles, Phil.	4	52	13.0	34	0
Barnes, Clev.	4	47	11.8	40	0
Martha, Pitt.	4	41	10.3	23	0
Shorter, Wash.	4	32	8.0	21	0
LeBeau, Det.	4	29	7.3	27	0
Gentry, Chi.	4	25	6.3	17	0
Logan, Balt.	4	22	5.5	11	0
Adderley, G. B.	4	16	4.0	t12	1
Robinson, G. B.	4	16	4.0	12	0
Stovall, St. L.	4	6	1.5	6	0
Calland, Atl.	5	106	35.3	t77	1
Houston, Clev.	3	97	32.3	t79	2
Sharockman, Minn.	3	94	31.3	37	0
Jordan, Dall.	5	85	28.3	40	1
Burkett, N. O.	3	57	19.0	23	0
Nobis, Atl.	3	57	19.0	t41	1
Russell, Pitt.	3	50	16.7	42	0
Buffone, Chi.	3	39	13.0	22	0
Keys, Pitt.-Minn.	3	38	12.7	30	0
Nitschke, G. B.	3	35	11.7	t20	1
Edwards, Dall.	6	34	11.3	t26	1
Logan, N. O.	3	21	7.0	18	0
Howell, Clev.	3	20	6.7	20	0
Shinnick, Balt.	3	20	6.7	17	0
Gonsoulin, S. F.	3	9	3.0	5	0
D. Smith, Wash.	3	0	0.0	0	0
Brewer, Clev.	2	75	37.5	t70	1
J. Johnson, S. F.	2	68	34.0	38	0
White, N. Y.	2	53	26.5	45	0
Campbell, Pitt.	2	52	26.0	30	0
Lucci, Det.	2	47	23.5	t31	1
Daniel, L. A.	2	45	22.5	35	0
Hackbart, Minn.	2	45	22.5	24	1
Thomas, Pitt.	2	39	19.5	33	0
Warwick, Minn.	2	36	18.0	19	0
Haymond, Balt.	2	33	16.5	33	0
F. Brown, Phil.	2	29	14.5	17	0
Caffey, G. B.	2	28	14.0	24	0
Hudlow, Atl.	2	25	12.5	21	0
Woodlief, L. A.	2	24	12.0	15	0
Medved, Phil.	2	23	11.5	23	0
B. Williams, St. L.	2	21	10.5	19	0
Lamson, L. A.	2	18	9.0	10	0
Wilcox, S. F.	2	17	8.5	17	0
Maher, Det.	2	14	7.0	14	0
Spiller, St. L.	2	13	6.5	13	0
Stukes, Balt.	2	13	6.5	13	0
Cornish, Chi.	2	10	5.0	6	0
Gaubatz, Balt.	2	10	5.0	5	0
Kassulke, Minn.	2	10	5.0	10	0
Huff, Wash.	2	8	4.0	5	0

	No.	Yds.	Avg.	Long	Tds.
Martin, Phil.	2	8	4.0	8	0
Eaton, N. Y.	2	7	3.5	7	0
Hand, Det.	2	6	3.0	t4	2
Burson, St. L.	2	0	0.0	0	0
Cross, L. A.	2	0	0.0	0	0
Gaechter, Dall.	2	0	0.0	0	0
Hohn, Pitt.	2	0	0.0	0	0

*—High for 1967.
†—1966 Leader.
t—Touchdown.

1967 PASS RECEIVING—INDIVIDUAL

	No.	Yds.	Avg.	Long	Tds.
†TAYLOR, WASH.	*70	990	14.1	t86	9
J. Smith, Wash.	67	849	12.7	43	12
Richardson, Balt.	63	860	13.7	t31	8
Mitchell, Wash.	60	866	14.4	t65	6
Hawkins, Phil.	59	*1265	21.4	t87	10
Rentzel, Dall.	58	996	17.2	t74	8
Smith, St. L.	56	1205	21.5	t76	9
Mackey, Balt.	55	686	12.5	t34	3
Dowler, G. B.	54	836	15.5	t57	4
Casey, L. A.	53	871	16.4	t57	8
Thomas, N. Y.	51	877	17.2	t48	9
Wilburn, Pitt.	51	767	15.0	t66	5
Abramowicz, N. O.	50	721	14.4	t80	6
Jones, N. Y.	49	1209	*24.7	t70	*13
Hayes, Dall.	49	998	20.4	t64	10
Conrad, St. L.	47	637	13.6	53	2
Witcher, S. F.	46	705	15.3	t63	3
Compton, Pitt.	42	507	12.1	40	1
Reeves, Dall.	39	490	12.6	t60	6
E. Green, Clev.	39	369	9.5	t41	2
Farr, Det.	39	317	8.1	31	3
Taylor, N. O.	38	251	6.6	27	0
Morrison, N. Y.	37	524	14.2	t59	7
Truax, L. A.	37	487	13.2	41	4
Josephson, L. A.	37	400	10.8	48	4
Ballman, Phil.	36	524	14.6	t67	6
Whitfield, Wash.	36	494	13.7	53	2
Dale, G. B.	35	738	21.1	t86	5
Matte, Balt.	35	496	14.2	t88	3
Woodeshick, Phil.	34	391	11.5	t43	4
Osborn, Minn.	34	272	8.0	29	1
Randle, S. F.	33	502	15.2	58	4
McDonald, Atl.	33	436	13.2	t75	4
Warfield, Clev.	32	702	21.9	t49	8
Collins, Clev.	32	500	15.6	33	7
Koy, N. Y.	32	212	6.6	24	1
Gordon, Chi.	31	534	17.2	t93	5
Crow, S. F.	31	373	12.0	t59	3
Coffey, Atl.	30	196	6.5	22	1
Jefferson, Pitt.	29	459	15.8	t58	4
Snow, L. A.	28	735	26.3	t80	8
D. Williams, St. L.	28	405	14.5	t49	5
Gambrell, St. L.	28	398	14.2	t48	2
Hawkins, Balt.	27	469	17.4	54	4
Bass, L. A.	27	212	7.9	30	1
Malinchak, Det.	26	397	15.3	43	4
Hilton, Pitt.	26	343	13.2	t43	5
Parks, S. F.	26	313	12.0	43	2
Ditka, Phil.	26	274	10.5	25	2
Lang, Phil.	26	201	7.7	19	3
Poage, N. O.	24	380	15.8	65	0
Simmons, N. O.-Atl.	23	312	13.6	30	2
Willard, S. F.	23	242	10.5	25	1
Flatley, Minn.	23	232	10.1	27	0

	No.	Yds.	Avg.	Long	Tds.
Anderson, G. B. _____	22	331	15.0	37	3
Gilliam, N. O. _____	22	264	12.0	35	1
Brown, Minn. _____	22	263	12.0	43	0
T. Brown, Phil. _____	22	202	9.2	41	1
Lorick, Balt. _____	22	189	8.6	34	0
Phillips, Minn. _____	21	352	16.8	42	3
Kelly, Phil. _____	21	345	16.4	59	4
Cogdill, Det. _____	21	322	15.3	t52	1
Windsor, S. F. _____	21	254	12.1	t55	2
Lewis, S. F. _____	21	218	10.4	t32	2
Nowatzke, Det. _____	21	145	6.9	t25	2
Ogden, N. O.-Atl. _____	20	327	16.4	t82	1
Kelly, Clev. _____	20	282	14.1	48	2
Roland, St. L. _____	20	269	13.5	41	1
Morris, Chi. _____	20	231	11.6	31	1
Norman, Dall. _____	20	220	11.0	39	2
Kramer, N. O. _____	20	207	10.4	17	2
Hall, N. O. _____	19	249	13.1	21	0
Gros, Pitt. _____	19	175	9.2	22	0
Hill, Balt. _____	19	156	8.2	33	0
Frederickson, N. Y. _____	19	153	8.1	29	0
Bull, Chi. _____	18	250	13.9	63	1
Perkins, Dall. _____	18	116	6.4	15	0
Roberts, N. O. _____	17	384	22.6	*96	3
Love, Wash. _____	17	248	14.6	35	1
Hoak, Pitt. _____	17	111	6.5	20	1
Perkins, Balt. _____	16	302	18.9	57	2
Sayers, Chi. _____	16	126	7.9	t32	1
Pitts, G. B. _____	15	210	14.0	84	0
Gautt, St. L. _____	15	202	13.5	32	1
Martin, Atl. _____	15	182	12.1	36	3
Smith, Clev. _____	14	211	15.1	t49	1
Schultz, N. O. _____	14	186	13.3	25	0
McKeever, Minn. _____	14	184	13.1	42	0
Wilson, G. B. _____	14	88	6.3	21	0
Washington, Minn. _____	13	384	29.5	t85	2
Moore, Balt. _____	13	153	11.8	37	0
Henderson, Det. _____	13	144	11.1	41	0
Cunningham, S. F. _____	13	121	9.3	29	0
Beasley, Minn. _____	13	120	9.2	16	4
Dunn, Atl. _____	13	111	8.5	21	0
Wheelwright, Atl.-N. O. _____	13	107	8.2	30	0
Ficcolo, Chi. _____	13	103	7.9	25	0
Mason, L. A. _____	13	70	5.4	24	0
Grabowski, G. B. _____	12	171	14.3	53	1
Shy, Pitt. _____	12	152	12.7	55	1
Denny, Chi. _____	12	113	9.4	19	0
Smith, Atl. _____	11	227	20.6	60	0
Berry, Balt. _____	11	167	15.2	40	1
Allen, Wash. _____	11	101	9.2	21	1
Studstill, Det. _____	10	162	16.2	t37	2
Barnes, Atl. _____	10	154	15.4	44	1
Fleming, G. B. _____	10	126	12.6	19	1
Crespino, N. Y. _____	10	125	12.5	24	1
Gibbons, Det. _____	10	107	10.7	21	0
Thurlow, Wash. _____	10	95	9.5	25	0
Moore, Atl. _____	10	74	7.4	21	0
McDonald, Wash. _____	10	60	6.0	18	0

*—High for 1967.
†—1966 Leader.
t—Touchdown.

1967 RUSHING—INDIVIDUAL

	Atts.	Yds.	Avg.	Long	Tds.
KELLY, CLEV. _____	*235	*1205	*5.1	t42	*11
Osborn, Minn. _____	215	972	4.5	*73	2
†Sayers, Chi. _____	186	880	4.7	70	7

	Atts.	Yds.	Avg.	Long	Tds.
Roland, St. L.	234	876	3.7	70	10
Farr, Det.	206	860	4.2	57	3
Perkins, Dall.	201	823	4.1	30	6
Josephson, L. A.	178	800	4.5	27	4
Coffey, Atl.	180	722	4.0	t20	4
E. Green, Clev.	145	710	4.9	t59	4
Koy, N. Y.	146	704	4.8	61	4
Woodeshick, Phil.	155	670	4.3	41	6
Matte, Balt.	147	636	4.3	30	9
Bass, L. A.	187	627	3.4	27	6
Brown, Minn.	185	610	3.3	29	5
Reeves, Dall.	173	603	3.5	32	5
Gautt, St. L.	142	573	4.0	30	1
Willard, S. F.	169	510	3.0	20	5
Crow, S. F.	113	479	4.2	39	2
Grabowski, G. B.	120	466	3.9	24	2
Wilson, G. B.	103	453	4.4	40	2
Lorick, Balt.	133	436	3.3	22	6
Anderson, G. B.	97	402	4.1	40	6
Taylor, N. O.	130	390	3.0	16	2
Whitfield, Wash.	91	384	4.2	44	1
Watkins, Det.	106	361	3.4	28	4
Lewis, S. F.	67	342	5.1	52	6
Shy, Pitt.	99	341	3.4	t33	4
Lang, Phil.	101	336	3.3	21	2
Piccolo, Chi.	87	317	3.6	31	0
Asbury, Pitt.	80	315	3.9	*73	4
Frederickson, N. Y.	97	311	3.2	17	2
Hill, Balt.	90	311	3.5	18	2
Tarkenton, N.Y.	44	306	7.0	22	2
Butler, Pitt.	90	293	3.3	24	0
Nowatzke, Det.	70	288	4.1	15	4
Concannon, Chi.	67	279	4.2	31	3
Allen, Wash.	77	262	3.4	30	3
Gros, Pitt.	72	252	3.5	23	1
Pitts, G. B.	77	247	3.2	30	6
Wheelwright, Atl.-N.O.	80	241	3.0	13	1
Marsh, Det.	58	229	3.9	25	2
McDonald, Wash.	52	223	4.3	t35	4
Mason, L. A.	63	213	3.4	16	0
Cunningham, S. F.	43	212	4.9	t64	2
Gabriel, L. A.	43	198	4.6	23	6
Mitchell, Wash.	61	189	3.1	16	1
Williams, G. B.	35	188	5.4	37	1
T. Brown, Phil.	53	179	3.4	t13	1
Bull, Chi.	61	176	2.9	11	0
Triplett, N. Y.	58	171	2.9	14	2
Kapp, Minn.	27	167	6.2	24	2
Morrison, N. Y.	36	161	4.5	11	2
Crenshaw, St. L.	44	149	3.4	23	0
Brodie, S. F.	20	147	7.4	15	1
Garrison, Dall.	24	146	6.1	26	0
Johnson, Atl.	24	144	6.0	t17	1
Hoak, Pitt.	52	142	2.7	11	1
Kilmer, N. O.	20	142	7.1	31	1
Moore, Balt.	42	132	3.1	21	4
Rector, Atl.	24	127	5.3	16	0
Barrington, N. O.	34	121	3.6	22	0
Schultz, N. O.	32	117	3.7	t22	2
Kurek, Chi.	37	112	3.0	13	0
Moore, Atl.	53	104	2.0	18	0
Minniear, N. Y.	35	98	2.8	13	1
Sweetan, Det.	17	93	5.5	18	1
Norman, Dall.	9	91	10.1	28	0
Starr, G. B.	21	90	4.3	23	0
Unitas, Balt.	22	89	4.0	13	0
Smith, St. L.	9	86	9.6	18	0
McCall, N. O.	21	86	4.1	t49	1
Ellison, L. A.	14	84	6.0	42	0

	Atts.	Yds.	Avg.	Long	Tds.
Larson, Wash.	25	84	3.4	34	1
Meredith, Dall.	28	84	3.0	16	0
Conjar, Clev.	20	78	3.9	16	0
Pietrosante, Clev.	10	73	7.3	31	0
Clarke, Dall.	4	72	18.0	t56	1
Felts, Det.	10	66	6.6	22	0
Shivers, St. L.	20	64	3.2	12	1
Dunn, Atl.	27	63	2.3	11	0
Jones, N. Y.	5	60	12.0	t46	1
Shy, Dall.	17	59	3.5	13	0
Ryan, Clev.	22	57	2.6	12	0
Mercein, G. B.	14	56	4.0	15	1

*—High for 1967.
†—1966 Leader.
t—Touchdown.
L—Lateral.

1967 PUNTING—INDIVIDUAL

	Stdg.	No.	Yards	Avg. Dist.	Long	Blkd.
LOTHRIDGE, ATL.	1	*87	*3801	*43.7	62	0
Green, Chi.	2	79	3392	42.9	68	0
McNeill, N. O.	3	74	3174	42.9	66	0
†Lee, Balt.	4	49	2075	42.3	68	0
Kilgore, L. A.	5	68	2872	42.2	68	2
Walden, Minn.	6	75	3117	41.6	76	0
Richter, Wash.	7	72	2976	41.3	58	0
Latourette, St. L.	8	62	2532	40.8	67	0
Villanueva, Dall.	9	67	2707	40.4	57	0
Baker, Phil.	10	61	2335	38.3	53	1
Elliott, Pitt.	11	72	2744	38.1	55	2
Spurrier, S. F.	12	73	2745	37.6	61	1
Barney, Det.	13	47	1757	37.4	55	0
Anderson, G. B.	14	65	2378	36.6	63	1
Collins, Clev.	15	57	2078	36.5	52	2
Koy, N. Y.	—	40	1509	37.7	54	0
Studstill, Det.	—	36	1602	44.5	*78	0
Morrall, N. Y.	—	15	472	31.5	43	1
Kelly, Clev.	—	10	407	40.7	51	0
Chandler, G. B.	—	1	31	31.0	31	0

*—High for 1967.
†—1966 Leader.
NOTE: Standing based on average distance. To qualify for championship rating a player must punt at least 42 times.

1967 KICKOFF RETURNS—INDIVIDUAL

	Stdg.	No.	Yds.	Avg.	Long	Tds.
WILLIAMS, G. B.	1	18	739	*41.1	*t104	*4
†Sayers, Chi.	2	16	603	37.7	t103	3
Gilliam, N. O.	3	16	481	30.1	t94	1
Vaughn, Det.	4	16	446	27.9	60	0
Cunningham, S. F.	5	31	826	26.6	94	0
Roberts, N. O.	6	28	737	26.3	t91	1
Davis, Clev.	7	27	708	26.2	63	0
Smith, Atl.	8	*39	*976	25.0	t99	1
Love, Wash.	9	17	422	24.8	t96	1
Ward, Clev.	10	22	546	24.8	*t104	1
Gordon, Chi.	11	16	397	24.8	32	0
Moore, Balt.	12	16	392	24.5	37	0
B. Williams, St. L.	13	24	583	24.3	38	0
Jones, Minn.	14	25	597	23.9	t96	1
Harris, Wash.	15	25	580	23.2	47	0
Bryant, St. L.	16	14	324	23.1	32	0
Shy, Pitt.	17	21	473	22.5	45	0
Hathcock, N. Y.	18	14	315	22.5	38	0

Grim, Minn.	19	22	493	22.4	46	0
Martha, Pitt.	20	18	403	22.4	32	0
Childs, N. Y.	21	29	603	20.8	48	0
Watkins, Det.	22	20	411	20.6	44	0
Garrison, Dall.	23	20	366	18.3	36	0
Ellison, L. A.	—	13	340	26.2	58	0
Haymond, Balt.	—	13	326	25.1	48	0
T. Brown, Phil.	—	13	301	23.2	41	0
Baynham, Dall.	—	12	331	27.6	37	0
Fitzgerald, N.Y.-Atl.	—	12	240	20.0	30	0
Tucker, L. A.	—	11	242	22.0	37	0
Anderson, G. B.	—	11	226	20.5	30	0
Hawkins, Phil.	—	10	250	25.0	46	0
Butler, Pitt.	—	10	223	22.3	32	0
Spiller, St. L.	—	10	219	21.9	41	0
Adderley, G. B.	—	10	207	20.7	37	0

*—High for 1967.
†—1966 Leader.
‡—Touchdown.
NOTE Standing based on average return. To qualify for championship rating
    a player must return at least 14 kickoffs.

AFL STATISTICS FOR 1967

1967 RUSHING—INDIVIDUAL

	Atts.	Yds.	Avg.	Long	Tds.
†NANCE, Bos.	*269	*1216	4.5	53	7
Granger, Hou.	236	1194	5.1	67	6
Garrett, K. C.	236	1087	4.6	58	9
Post, S. D.	161	663	4.1	†67	7
Hubbert, S. D.	116	643	*5.5	*†80	2
Lincoln, Buff.	159	601	3.8	28	4
Daniels, Oak.	130	575	4.4	52	4
Dixon, Oak.	153	559	3.7	40	5
Campbell, Ho.	110	511	4.6	42	4
Carlton, Buff.	107	467	4.4	21	3
Boozer, N. Y.	119	442	3.7	48	*10
McClinton, K. C.	97	392	4.0	34	2
Little, Den.	130	381	2.9	14	1
Banaszak, Oak.	68	376	5.5	47	1
Haynes, Mia.-N.Y.	72	346	4.8	†65	2
Mitchell, Den.	82	308	3.8	35	0
Coan, K. C.	63	275	4.4	38	4
Mitchell, Mia.	83	269	3.2	22	3
Hickey, Den.	73	263	3.6	20	4
Hayes, Den.	85	255	3.0	18	4
Mathis, N. Y.	78	243	3.1	18	4
Snell, N. Y.	61	207	3.4	13	0
Blanks, Hou.	66	206	3.1	16	1
Harper, Mia.	41	197	4.8	†37	1
Price, Miami	46	179	3.9	38	1
Garron, Bos.	46	163	3.5	20	0
Griese, Mia.	37	157	4.2	22	1
Joe, N. Y.	37	154	4.2	26	2
Hagberg, Oak.	44	146	3.3	11	2
Smolinski, N. Y.	64	139	2.2	10	1
Beathard, Hou.	32	133	4.2	23	1
G. Thomas, K. C.	35	133	3.8	19	1
Auer, Miami	44	128	2.9	23	1
Todd, Oak.	29	116	4.0	16	2
Smith, S. D.	22	115	5.2	16	1
Lamonica, Oak.	22	110	5.0	26	4
Hadl, S. D.	37	107	2.9	26	3
Cappadona, Bo.	28	100	3.6	11	0
Burnett, Buff.	45	96	2.1	18	0
Foster, S. D.	38	78	2.1	13	0
Lowe, S. D.	28	71	2.5	21	1
Dawson, K. C.	20	68	3.4	24	0

	Atts.	Yds.	Avg.	Long	Tds.
Parilli, Bos.	14	61	4.4	18	0
Seiple, Miami	3	58	19.3	34	0
Bivins, Buff.	15	58	3.9	43	0
Kemp, Buff.	36	58	1.6	14	2

*—High for 1967.
†—1966 Leader.
‡—Touchdown.

1967 SCORING—INDIVIDUAL

	Td.R.	Td.P.	Td.Ret.	Tot. Tds.	XP	XPM	2-Pt. PAT	FG	FGA	Tot. Pts.
BLANDA, Oakland	0	0	0	0	*56	1	0	20	30	*116
Stenerud, K. C.	0	0	0	0	45	0	0	*21	36	108
†Cappelletti, Bos.	0	3	0	3	29	1	0	16	31	95
VanRaaphorst, S.D.	0	0	0	0	45	0	0	15	30	90
J. Turner, N. Y.	0	0	0	0	36	*3	0	17	32	87
Boozer, N. Y.	*10	3	0	*13	0	0	0	0	0	78
Mercer, Buff.	0	0	0	0	25	0	0	16	27	73
Taylor, K. C.	1	*11	0	12	0	0	0	0	0	72
Wittenborn, Hous.	0	0	0	0	30	0	0	14	28	72
Denson, Denver	0	*11	0	11	0	0	0	0	0	66
Maynard, N. Y.	0	10	0	10	0	0	1	0	0	62
Cannon, Oak.	0	10	0	10	0	0	0	0	0	60
Frazier, S. D.	0	10	0	10	0	0	0	0	0	60
Garrett, K. C.	9	1	0	10	0	0	0	0	0	60
Alworth, S. D.	0	9	0	9	0	0	0	0	0	54
Granger, Hous.	6	3	0	9	0	0	0	0	0	54
Lincoln, Buff.	4	5	0	9	0	0	0	0	0	54
Nance, Boston	7	1	0	8	0	0	0	0	0	48
Post, San Diego	7	1	0	8	0	0	0	0	0	48
Mathis, N. Y.	4	3	0	7	0	0	2	0	0	46
Dixon, Oakland	5	2	0	7	0	0	0	0	0	42
Humphreys, Denver	0	0	0	0	18	1	0	7	15	39
Lusteg, Miami	0	0	0	0	18	0	0	7	12	39
Sauer, N. Y.	0	6	0	6	0	0	1	0	0	38
Cambpbell, Hous.	4	2	0	6	0	0	0	0	0	36
Daniels, Oakland	4	2	0	6	0	0	0	0	0	36
Miller, Oakland	0	6	0	6	0	0	0	0	0	36
Wells, Oakland	0	6	0	6	0	0	0	0	0	36
Arbanas, K. C.	0	5	0	5	0	0	0	0	0	30
Biletnikoff, Oak.	0	5	0	5	0	0	0	0	0	30
Crabtree, Denver	0	5	0	5	0	0	0	0	0	30
Garron, Boston	0	5	0	5	0	0	0	0	0	30
Hickey, Denver	4	1	0	5	0	0	0	0	0	30
Whalen, Boston	0	5	0	5	0	0	0	0	0	30
Hayes, Denver	4	0	0	4	0	0	0	0	0	26
Coan, K. C.	4	0	0	4	0	0	0	0	0	24
Graham, Boston	0	4	0	4	0	0	0	0	0	24
Harper, Miami	1	3	0	4	0	0	0	0	0	24
Hubbert, S. D.	2	2	0	4	0	0	0	0	0	24
Lamonica, Oak.	4	0	0	4	0	0	0	0	0	24
Mitchell, Miami	3	1	0	4	0	0	0	0	0	24
Powell, Buffalo	0	4	0	4	0	0	0	0	0	24
Smolinski, N. Y.	1	3	0	4	0	0	0	0	0	24
McClinton, K. C.	2	1	0	3	0	0	1	0	0	20
Auer, Miami	1	2	0	3	0	0	0	0	0	18
Burford, K. C.	0	3	0	3	0	0	0	0	0	18
Carlton, Buffalo	3	0	0	3	0	0	0	0	0	18
Duncan, San Diego	0	0	*3	3	0	0	0	0	0	18
Farr, Houston	0	0	*3	3	0	0	0	0	0	18
Hadl, San Diego	3	0	0	3	0	0	0	0	0	18
Hagberg, Oakland	2	1	0	3	0	0	0	0	0	18
Houston, Hous.	0	0	*3	3	0	0	0	0	0	18
Moreau, Miami	0	3	0	3	0	0	0	0	0	18
G. Thomas, K. C.	1	2	0	3	0	0	0	0	0	18
Trull, Boston	3	0	0	3	0	0	0	0	0	18
Kemp, Buffalo	2	0	0	2	0	0	1	0	0	14
Banaszak, Oak.	1	1	0	2	0	0	0	0	0	12
Blanks, Houston	1	1	0	2	0	0	0	0	0	12
Clancy, Miami	0	2	0	2	0	0	0	0	0	12
Connors, Oakland	0	0	2	2	0	0	0	0	0	12

	Td.R.	Td.P.	Td.Ret.	Tot. Tds.	XP	XPM	2-Pt. PAT	FG	FGA	Tot. Pts.
Costa, Buffalo _____	0	2	0	2	0	0	0	0	0	12
Garrison, S. D. _____	0	2	0	2	0	0	0	0	0	12
Haynes, Miami _____	0	2	0	2	0	0	0	0	0	12
Janik, Buffalo _____	0	0	2	2	0	0	0	0	0	12
Joe, New York _____	2	0	0	2	0	0	0	0	0	12
Lammons, N. Y. _____	0	2	0	2	0	0	0	0	0	12
Ledbetter, Hou.-Buff.	0	2	0	2	0	0	0	0	0	12
Little, Denver _____	1	0	1	2	0	0	0	0	0	12
MacKinnon, S. D. __	0	2	0	2	0	0	0	0	0	12
Masters, Buff. _____	0	2	0	2	0	0	0	0	0	12
Mingo, Miami _____	0	0	0	0	9	0	0	1	6	12
Pitts, K. C. _____	1	1	0	2	0	0	0	0	0	12
Powers, Oakland ___	0	0	2	2	0	0	0	0	0	12
Price, Miami _____	1	1	0	2	0	0	0	0	0	12
Richardson, K. C. __	0	2	0	2	0	0	0	0	0	12
Todd, Oakland _____	2	0	0	2	0	0	0	0	0	12
Twilley, Miami _____	0	2	0	2	0	0	0	0	0	12
Wilson, Denver _____	0	0	2	2	0	0	0	0	0	12

*—High for 1967.
†—1966 Leader.
SAFETIES SCORED BY: Buoniconti and Hunt, Boston; Jackson and White, Denver; Birdwell, Oakland. Kansas City scored automatic safety.

1967 KICKOFF RETURNS—INDIVIDUAL

	Stdg.	No.	Yds.	Avg.	Long	Tds.
MOORE, Houston _____	1	14	405	*28.9	t92	*1
N. Smith, K. C. _____	2	*41	*1148	28.0	*t106	*1
Little, Denver _____	3	35	942	26.9	60	0
Post, San Diego _____	4	15	371	24.7	50	0
Tolbert, San Diego _____	5	18	441	24.5	45	0
Bivins, Buffalo _____	6	16	380	23.8	55	0
Neff, Miami _____	7	15	351	23.4	69	0
Christy, New York _____	8	23	521	22.7	33	0
Haynes, Miami-N.Y. _____	9	26	569	21.9	51	0
Janclk, Houston _____	10	16	349	21.8	49	0
Smith, Buffalo _____	11	16	346	21.6	64	0
Grayson, Oakland _____	12	19	405	21.3	29	0
Auer, Miami _____	13	21	441	21.0	47	0
Cunningham, Boston ___	14	30	627	20.9	41	0
Bellino, Boston _____	15	18	357	19.8	32	0
C. King, Buffalo _____	—	12	316	26.3	38	0
Sherman, Oakland _____	—	12	279	23.3	49	0
Leo, Boston _____	—	11	232	21.1	31	0
Boozer, New York _____	—	11	213	19.4	28	0
Duncan, San Diego _____	—	9	231	25.7	60	0
Brannan, New York _____	—	9	204	22.7	47	0
Carwell, Houston _____	—	8	164	20.5	27	0
Mitchell, Denver _____	—	8	164	20.5	32	0
Lowe, San Diego _____	—	8	145	18.1	29	0

*—High for 1967.
†—1966 Leader.
t—Touchdown.
L—Lateral.
NOTE: Standing computed on the basis of average per return. To qualify for championship a player must return at least 14 kickoffs.

1967 PASS RECEIVING—INDIVIDUAL

	No.	Yds.	Avg.	Long	Tds.
SAUER, N. Y. _____	*75	1189	15.9	t61	6
Maynard, N. Y. _____	71	*1434	*20.2	t75	10
Clancy, Mia. _____	67	868	13.0	t44	2
Taylor, K. C. _____	59	958	16.2	t71	*11
Dixon, Oak. _____	59	563	9.5	48	2
Frazier, S. D. _____	57	922	16.2	t72	10

	No.	Yds.	Avg.	Long	Tds.
†Alworth, S. D.	52	1010	19.4	t71	9
Denson, Den.	46	899	19.5	t68	*11
Crabtree, Den.	46	716	15.6	t76	5
Garrett, K. C.	46	261	5.7	t34	1
Lammons, N. Y.	45	515	11.4	.61	2
Garrison, S. D.	44	772	17.5	62	2
Graham, Bos.	41	606	14.8	*t79	4
Lincoln, Buff.	41	558	13.6	t60	5
Biletnikoff, Oak.	40	376	21.9	72	5
Costa, Buff.	39	726	18.6	t63	2
Whalen, Bos.	39	651	16.7	t41	5
Miller, Oak.	38	537	14.1	38	6
Cappelletti, Bos.	35	397	11.3	35	3
Moreau, Miami	34	410	12.1	43	3
Cannon, Oak.	32	629	19.7	t64	10
Post, S. D.	32	278	8.7	t66	1
Granger, Hou.	31	300	9.7	t43	3
Garron, Bos.	30	507	16.9	66	5
McClinton, K. C.	26	219	8.4	25	1
Mathis, N. Y.	25	429	17.2	38	3
Burford, K. C.	25	389	15.6	55	3
Dubenion, Buff.	25	384	15.4	42	0
Twilley, Miami	24	314	13.1	38	2
Frazier, Hou.	23	253	11.0	53	1
Nance, Bos.	22	196	8.9	36	1
Smolinski, N. Y.	21	177	8.4	22	3
Powell, Buff.	20	346	17.3	t37	4
Arbanas, K. C.	20	295	14.8	43	5
Masters, Buff.	20	274	13.7	28	2
Hubbert, S. D.	19	214	11.3	49	2
Taylor, Hou.	18	233	12.9	23	1
Auer, Miami	18	218	12.1	t68	2
Mitchell, Miami	18	133	7.4	38	1
Campbell, Hou.	17	136	8.0	32	2
Daniels, Oak.	16	222	13.9	t40	2
Banaszak, Oak.	16	192	12.0	72	1
Haynes, Miami	16	100	6.3	22	0
Colclough, Bos.	14	263	18.8	52	0
Wells, Oak.	13	302	23.2	t50	6
Ledbetter, Hou.-Buff.	13	204	15.7	t60	2
Hayes, Den.	13	125	9.6	24	0
G. Thomas, K. C.	13	99	7.6	27	2
Richardson, K. C.	12	312	26.0	t56	2
Boozer, N. Y.	12	205	17.1	t49	3
Burrell, Hou.	12	193	16.1	39	0
Noonan, Miami	12	141	11.8	32	1
Harper, Miami	11	212	19.3	t40	3
Beer, Den.	11	155	14.1	29	1
Reed, Hou.	11	144	13.1	20	1
Burnett, Buff.	11	114	10.4	38	0
Hagberg, Oak.	11	114	10.4	25	1
Blanks, Hou.	11	93	8.5	t39	1
Snell, N. Y.	11	54	4.9	21	0
Carpenter, Mia.	10	127	12.7	42	0

*—High for 1967.
†—1966 Leader.
t—Touchdown.

1967 PUNTING—INDIVIDUAL

	Stdg.	No.	Yards	Avg. Dist.	Long	Blkd.
†SCARPITTO, Denver	1	*105	*4713	*44.9	*73	1
Eischeld, Oakland	2	76	3364	44.3	62	1
Maguire, Buffalo	3	77	3320	43.1	64	0
Norton, Buffalo	4	71	3025	42.6	58	1
Wilson, K. C.	5	41	1739	42.4	59	1
Johnson, New York	6	65	2734	42.1	60	0
Seiple, Miami	7	70	2909	41.6	70	1

Swanson, Boston	8	65	2632	40.5	62	0
Redman, San Diego	9	58	2147	37.0	56	0
Walker, Kansas City	—	19	736	38.7	56	0
Cordell, San Diego	—	3	145	48.3	52	0
Hadl, San Diego	—	2	70	35.0	46	0
Carolan, Kansas City	—	1	42	42.0	42	0

*—High for 1967.
†—1966 Leader.
NOTE: Standing computed on the basis of average distance. To qualify for
championship rating a player must punt at least 28 times.

1967 INTERCEPTIONS—INDIVIDUAL

	No.	Yds.	Avg.	Long	Tds.
FARR, Hou.	*10	*264	26.4	67	*3
JANIK, Buff.	*10	222	22.2	46	2
WESTMORELAND, Mia.	*10	127	12.7	29	1
Sellers, Den.	7	78	11.1	47	1
Brown, Oak.	7	33	4.7	t25	1
Powers, Oak.	6	154	25.7	70	2
F. Smith, K. C.	6	150	25.0	57	0
Norton, Hou.	6	73	12.2	26	1
Grantham, N. Y.	5	77	15.4	36	0
†Hunt, K. C.	5	71	14.2	39	0
Atkinson, N. Y.	5	59	11.8	36	0
Byrd, Buff.	5	25	5.0	12	0
†Robinson, K. C.	5	17	3.4	10	0
Wilson, Den.	4	153	38.3	t70	2
Houston, Hou.	4	151	37.8	78	2
Williams, Oak.	4	96	24.0	37	0
Webb, Bos.	4	91	22.8	41	0
Mitchell, K. C.	4	88	22.0	55	1
Bell, K. C.	4	82	20.5	t32	1
Lentz, Den.	4	72	18.0	47	0
Grayson, Oak.	4	63	15.8	23	0
E. Thomas, K. C.	4	60	15.0	t57	1
Beverly, N. Y.	4	54	13.5	28	0
Sample, N. Y.	4	53	13.3	t41	1
Hudson, N. Y.	4	38	9.5	18	0
Bramlett, Miami	4	35	8.8	22	0
Warren, Miami	4	22	5.5	17	0
Wright, Den.	4	22	5.5	8	0
Buoniconti, Bos.	4	7	1.8	7	0
Hicks, Hou.	3	122	40.7	62	0
Schottenheimer, Buff.	3	88	29.3	t45	1
Petrella, Miami	3	67	22.3	28	0
Shonta, Bos.	3	57	19.0	28	0
Beauchamp, S. D.	3	44	14.7	28	0
Connors, Oak.	3	42	14.0	t30	1
Baird, N. Y.	3	27	9.0	17	0
Mitchell, Bos.	3	9	3.0	9	0
Duncan, S. D.	2	100	50.0	* 100	1
Graham, S. D.	2	76	38.0	t68	1
Sykes, Den.	2	29	14.5	29	0
Redman, S. D.	2	26	13.0	23	0
Edgerson, Buff.	2	25	12.5	25	0
Saimes, Buff.	2	14	7.0	14	0
Huard, Den.	2	12	6.0	9	0
Williamson, Oak.	2	9	4.5	6	0
McCloughan, Oak.	2	7	3.5	7	0
Richter, Den.	2	6	3.0	6	0
Allen, S. D.	2	2	1.0	2	0

*—High for 1967.
†—1966 Leader.
t—Touchdown.
L—Lateral.

1967 PASSING—INDIVIDUAL

	Std.	Att.	Comp.	Pct. Comp.	Yds. Gain	Tds	Long	Had Int.	Pct. Int.	Avg. Gain
LAMONICA, Oakland __	1	425	220	51.8	3228	*30	72	20	*4.7	7.60
†Dawson, Kan. City __	2	357	206	*57.7	2651	24	t71	17	4.8	7.43
Namath, New York __	3	*491	*258	52.5	*4007	26	t75	28	5.7	*8.16
Hadl, San Diego ____	4	427	217	50.8	3365	24	t72	22	5.2	7.88
Griese, Miami _____	5	331	166	50.2	2005	15	t68	18	5.4	6.06
Parilli, Boston _____	6	344	161	46.8	2317	19	*t79	24	7.0	6.74
Tensi, Denver _____	7	325	131	40.3	1915	16	t76	17	5.2	5.89
Kemp, Buffalo _____	8	369	161	43.6	2503	14	t63	26	7.0	6.78
Beathard, K.C.-Hou. __	9	231	94	40.7	1114	9	t43	*14	6.1	4.82
Norton, Miami _____	__	133	53	39.8	596	1	32	9	6.8	4.48
Lee, Hou.-K.C. _____	__	91	42	46.2	414	3	53	6	6.6	4.55
Trull, Hou.-Bos. ____	__	92	31	33.7	480	1	52	7	7.6	5.22
Flores, Buffalo _____	__	64	22	34.4	260	0	59	8	12.5	4.06
LeClair, Denver _____	__	45	19	42.2	275	1	48	1	2.2	6.11
Blanda, Oakland ____	__	38	15	39.5	285	3	t50	3	7.9	7.50
Taliaferro, N. York __	__	20	11	55.0	96	1	t20	1	5.0	4.80
Stephenson, S. D. ___	__	26	11	42.3	117	2	21	2	7.7	4.50

*—High for 1967.
†—1966 Leader.
t—Touchdown.
NOTE: Standing based on completion percentage, touchdown passes, percent of interceptions and average gain per attempt.
To qualify for championship rating a player must throw a minimum of 140 passes.

1967 PUNT RETURNS—INDIVIDUAL

	Stdg.	No.	F.C.	Yards	Avg.	Long	Tds.
LITTLE, Denver _____	1	16	6	270	*16.9	t72	*1
Bird, Oakland _____	2	*46	*16	*612	13.3	*78	0
†Duncan, San Diego __	3	36	6	434	12.1	50	0
Baird, New York _____	4	25	3	219	8.8	33	0
Bellino, Boston _____	5	15	8	129	8.6	18	0
N. Smith, K. C. _____	6	26	9	212	8.2	59	0
Cunningham, Boston __	7	17	5	105	6.2	44	0
Christy, New York ___	8	16	0	83	5.2	16	0
Byrd, Buffalo _____	9	30	5	142	4.7	19	0
Rutkowski, Buffalo __	10	15	4	43	2.9	12	0
Carwell, Houston ____	__	9	4	154	17.1	54	0
Auer, Miami _____	__	9	1	42	4.7	16	0
Lewis, New York ____	__	7	0	24	3.4	11	0
Johnson, Boston _____	__	6	1	124	20.7	52	0
Haynes, Miami _____	__	6	2	37	6.2	20	0
Neff, Miami _____	__	6	3	34	5.7	15	0
Jancik, Houston _____	__	6	2	19	3.2	19	0
Moore, Houston _____	__	5	1	82	16.4	46	0

*—High for 1967.
†—1966 Leader.
t—Touchdown.
NOTE: Standing computed on the basis of average per return. To qualify for championship rating a player must return at least 14 punts.